Brunel's Great Eastern

'The ship that changed everything'

Hirotatsu Kambara, Tsuneishi

'Brunel: engineer and showman'

HRH Prince Edward, Earl of Wessex

Brunel's Great Eastern

Eric Kentley and Robert Hulse

Foreword by Joanna Lumley

The Brunel Museum

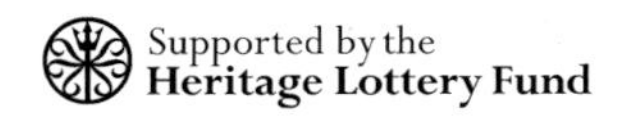

First published in
Great Britain in 2016 by
The Brunel Museum

British Library
Cataloguing-in-Publication Data
A catalogue record for this book is available from the British Library

ISBN 978-0-9504361-3-5

Design by Isambard Thomas

Typeset in Linotype Frutiger

Printed by Graphicom, Verona

TITLE PAGE ILLUSTRATION
Building the 'Great Leviathan'
by William Parrott.
On the right hand side of the river are Sir Christopher Wren's buildings for the Royal Naval Hospital and the Royal Observatory.

Photographic credits

2–3 © National Maritime Museum, London; 9 Private Collection; 14–15 Isambard Thomas; 18 National Portrait Gallery; 20 © National Maritime Museum, London; 21 © Science Museum / Science & Society Picture Library; 22 The Institution of Mechanical Engineers / Mary Evans; 25 By courtesy of the Brunel Institute – a collaboration of the ss Great Britain Trust and the University of Bristol; 28–29 © Science Museum / Science & Society Picture Library; 30 Robert Hulse (t); Isambard Thomas (b); 30 Private Collection; 32 Private Collection; 34–35 Private Collection; 36 © Illustrated London News Ltd / Mary Evans; 37, 38, 41 The Institution of Mechanical Engineers / Mary Evans; 42–43 © National Maritime Museum, Greenwich, London; 44 © Science Museum/ Science & Society Picture Library; 48 © National Railway Museum/ Science & Society Picture Library; 51 Mary Evans Picture Library; 53 By courtesy of the ss Great Britain Trust; 54 Eric Kentley; 55 (tr) © National Maritime Museum, London; 55 (bl) © Science Museum / Science & Society Picture Library; 57 © Illustrated London News Ltd / Mary Evans; 58 Mary Evans Picture Library; 59 © Illustrated London News Ltd / Mary Evans; 60 Mary Evans Picture Library; 61 Courtesy Memorial University Libraries, St. John's, Canada; 62, 63 Mary Evans Picture Library; 64 © National Maritime Museum,London; 67 © National Maritime Museum, London; 69 Mary Evans / Roger Worsley Archive; 71 © National Maritime Museum, London; 75 Mary Evans Picture Library; 77–78 © Illustrated London News Ltd / Mary Evans; 80–81 Courtesy SLV State Library of Victoria

Shipbuilding today

The Industrial Revolution prompted rapid development in land and marine transportation in Victorian times. Isambard Kingdom Brunel was at the centre of this period of massive change, particularly in relation to shipbuilding. He built the biggest ship in the world three times: the SS *Great Western*, SS *Great Britain* and finally SS *Great Eastern*. He was the pioneer of large iron-hulled steamships for intercontinental transport.

Brunel's first significant contribution to shipping was to demonstrate that the steam engine was viable for ocean voyaging. Secondly he pioneered the development of the propeller-driven ship. Thirdly he introduced the massive iron ship with a double hull, strengthened by watertight bulkheads. These were the foundations for modern shipbuilding, contributing to the United Kingdom's position as world leader. Today, Japanese techniques in welding and block construction have produced large capacity economical ships, like Brunel's, and in 1957, Japan became the leading shipbuilding nation.

The *Great Eastern* was the most innovative vessel of the age, which Brunel described as built like a bridge in order to be strong enough not to sag. The huge ship was built on one site in east London, but Tsuneishi has developed modular construction to build across a network of yards and technical sites. Components are then assembled on site like the trestle bridges on Brunel's Great Western Railway. Brunel moved components on railways he had built, using trains he had designed. Similarly, Tsuneishi ship out their components in their own sea containers on their own ships

Brunel appreciated that the shape of a ship's hull is crucial to her performance. He would have been fascinated by model experiments Tsuneishi has undertaken in co-operation with Hiroshima University, which refined the shape of the bow, reducing wave resistance by up to five per cent and so reducing fuel costs.

Interestingly, modern computers have only been able to improve the efficiency of the propeller Brunel designed for the *Great Britain* by one per cent. Only recently have Japanese designers found ways to improve propeller performance, by attaching extra fins in front to affect rotational flows. The global maritime industry is now highly developed, highly designed and highly efficient. Today over 95% of our goods travel by sea, and much is due to the pioneering work of Isambard Kingdom Brunel. This his last ship and the ship that changed everything.

I.K. Brunel leaning on the chains of one of the checking drums used in the launch of the *Great Eastern*, photographed by Robert Howlett, November 1857

Mr. Hirotatsu Kambara
President, TSUNEISHI HOLDINGS CORPORATION

Prof. Dr. Kuniji Kose
Professor Emeritus, Hiroshima University

Absolutely Fabulous Ship

Like Prometheus, Isambard Kingdom Brunel is held in chains forever, but on the Isle of Dogs. The chains were for launching Leviathan his monster ship, and this iconic photograph was taken by Robert Howlett in 1857. Here is the engineer triumphant, and since the London Olympics, the Industrial Revolution personified. The fabulous opening ceremony peopled the stadium with stove pipe hats, led by Kenneth Branagh, and they built factories and forged chains in smoke and in flames, in furnace and in cauldron. The Victorians' favourite word for gigantic, world changing, world-shocking engineering was Promethean, and Brunel in front of his chains is masterful and commanding.

I am standing where Promethean Brunel stood, where his great ship was built in the yards of John Scott Russell. Unfortunately, everything went wrong: the ship stuck on the ramps, the drum of chains in the famous photograph broke loose and an iron pole cartwheeled across the yard and impaled a labourer. The ship was finally pushed inch by inch into the river, but a merciless public nicknamed her 'the ship that doesn't like the water'. Brunel at the height of his powers, collapses and is carried to his London home and his death bed. High drama, and beneath the triumphal pose a real tragedy is being played out. There are also elements of farce…

The ship and the chains are long gone, but remnants of the launch ways still stretch down to the Thames, and they are monumental: in fact the site has been Scheduled as a Ancient Monument in recognition of its national importance. Today the site is quiet, but the clamour here, at the biggest construction site in the world, must have been fearsome. Teams of men hammered three million rivets into the hull of the *Great Eastern, Leviathan* or *Sea Monster* as she was also nicknamed. She dominated the flat grey surroundings here on the Isle of Dogs.

The river was almost as noisy as the shipyard. In Brunel's day this was the busiest river in the world and the biggest traffic jam in the world. The trade of the world came up the Thames, and there were three thousand tall masted ships in the river every day. The river was so congested, it took longer to get cargo across the Thames than it took to get across the Atlantic. The tall masts have been replaced by funnels, thanks to Brunel, and even the funnels have gone now, but for me this is still the river Joseph Conrad described as 'leading to the uttermost ends of the earth'.

The *Great Eastern* was built for the run to India, and that is where I was born, a year before Independence, in Srinagar high in the Kashmiri hills. Before I could start to appreciate my stunning luck at being born in such a paradise, all the British were required to leave. We trundled down to Bombay and boarded the *Franconia* bound for Southampton. Being a soldier's family meant that we travelled on troopships to and from the Far East. Later we were to sail with the *Windrush*, the *Dilwara* and the *Empire Orwell*, grand names for dear old tin ships, some requisitioned from the Germans after the war, with the taps marked Heiss and Kalt, all smelling of Vaseline and covered with thick gloss paint.

It took five weeks to reach Hong Kong, then four weeks to Singapore where we disembarked to catch the train to Kuala Lumpur. Every Sunday on board ship we sang " For Those in Peril on the Sea" in the dining room which had been changed into a temporary church. We washed in tin baths in sea water and showered with fresh water to rinse away the salt. Every day we had an orange to eat; we looked forward to the Suez Canal, where a pilot would be brought out to the ship by motor launch, climbing aboard by a lowered ladder to steer us through the canal's narrow banks into or out of the Mediterranean.

Long stretches at sea were charted on a map we inspected daily. It seemed to us that we could smell land long before it was sighted: Colombo's spicy breezes, Aden's deserts and the cold shingle and concrete of Southampton. The ships were without frills: deck quoits and canasta were the high spots for adults while fancy dress competitions and weekly cartoon films kept the children happy.

The order of ports was this from Hong Kong: Singapore, Colombo, Aden, Port Said, Malta, Gibraltar and then, after the ghastly Bay of Biscay, Southampton. Today, thirty days seems to be a very long time to cross the world compared with air travel, but I would not have traded those fabulous journeys for all the tea in China.

The old sailing ships and the *Great Eastern,* without the benefit of Suez, had a rather different order of ports. Under sail, the journey took ninety to a hundred days, but steamers like Brunel's were much faster and some advertised the journey as just fifty four days. Steamships were not chasing trade winds, but they must stop to take on coal. And like the sailing ships, they must go south and further south, round the Cape of Good Hope into the Indian Ocean.

At seven hundred feet long, Brunel's steamship was different because she was so big, so big she had to be launched sideways. One of her nicknames was 'floating coal bunker', and she was big enough to steam from London to India - and back again - without refuelling. This not only saved money, it saved time. Coal bought from a coaling station had to be shipped out there, so was bought at a premium, sometimes ten times the price of good, cheap Welsh coal.

Brunel's ship is probably the last really posh old ship. Disappointingly there is no evidence for the favourite old acronym Port Out Starboard Home, but wealthy passengers certainly chose cabins on the port side to avoid the afternoon sun on the long journey south. Brunel's ship was mostly posh because the first-class passengers travelled in unheard of luxury. The food on the *Great Eastern* was superb, the public rooms were decorated in the height of fashion and were unusually spacious. Travel was more dangerous then, but for those who had money it was luxurious.

When the Suez Canal opened in 1869 there was suddenly a new and different passage to India, and one closer to the route we took on the troopships. Travellers could avoid the Bay of Biscay by taking a channel ferry, a train to Marseille and a steamer to Port Said and then Suez. The *Great Eastern*, designed to cut days off the journey to India, was too big to pass through Suez, and so in a sense her fate was sealed by another extraordinary piece of engineering. However the great ship beat them all in the end: the fastest way to send anything to India was by telegraph and the *Great Eastern* laid the cable across the Indian Ocean. Brunel's ship brought two worlds closer together.

Brunel built three ships, and each was important, but the *Great Eastern* was his last and greatest. The biggest ship in the world and the biggest ship in the world for half a century. When the *Great Eastern* was launched, she was six times bigger than anything else afloat, an engineering triumph, and a ship that heralded in new trading patterns and a communications revolution that has changed the world. The *Great Eastern* was not a commercial success, but she is the ancestor of the super tankers, the giant container ships and the bulk carriers that carry most of our goods today. People seemed to love her, and from the day construction started on the Isle of Dogs to her final voyage to the breaker's yard in Birkenhead, they turned out in force to see the marvel of the age.

Before the *Great Eastern* was broken up, people came to the ship for entertainment, for music hall and dance. When she first arrived in America, she was the event of the New York season: stalls and sideshows filled the ship and trapeze artists performed on the main deck. Later in Liverpool, acts included Tom Coyne eccentric comedian, Cyrus and Maude musical grotesques, Mons Derkaro the Japanese Wonder, W.H. Vane the banjo king, various burlesque artists and Miss Nelly Fletcher skipping rope dancer.

So the *Great Eastern* was a showboat and Brunel was a showman as well as a world changer. He was a polymath, difficult to define: civil engineer, marine engineer, mechanical engineer, chemical engineer. He wished to be 'the first engineer and an example for all future ones'. He was a stylish man, a man who liked to cut a figure and patron of the arts as well as man of science. He enjoyed the theatre, and as a young man proudly took actress Fanny Kemble on a tour of his first project, the Thames Tunnel, just up the river from where I'm standing. For his elegant London home, he commissioned paintings illustrating the plays of William Shakespeare and they hung in what became known as his 'Shakespeare Room'. The most famous is Sir Edwin Landseer's fantastical painting for *A Midsummer's Night Dream:* on a grassy bank, Titania, Queen of the Faeries, sits with Bottom the weaver, and on top of his ass's head sits a daisy chain.

The chain in the photograph on the Isle of Dogs is better known, and this is the persistent image of engineer Isambard Kingdom Brunel, but I like to remember his whimsical side and the daisy chain. I like to remember the actress, the fairground entertainments on the *Great Eastern* and the waltzes in the Thames Tunnel, because ultimately Brunel was a romantic. Everything he did, by land or by sea, he did with style and flare and showmanship, and we see this in the famous last image. He built the ship, he changed the world, he held the stage - but sometimes he made daisy chains...

Joanna Lumley
London 2016

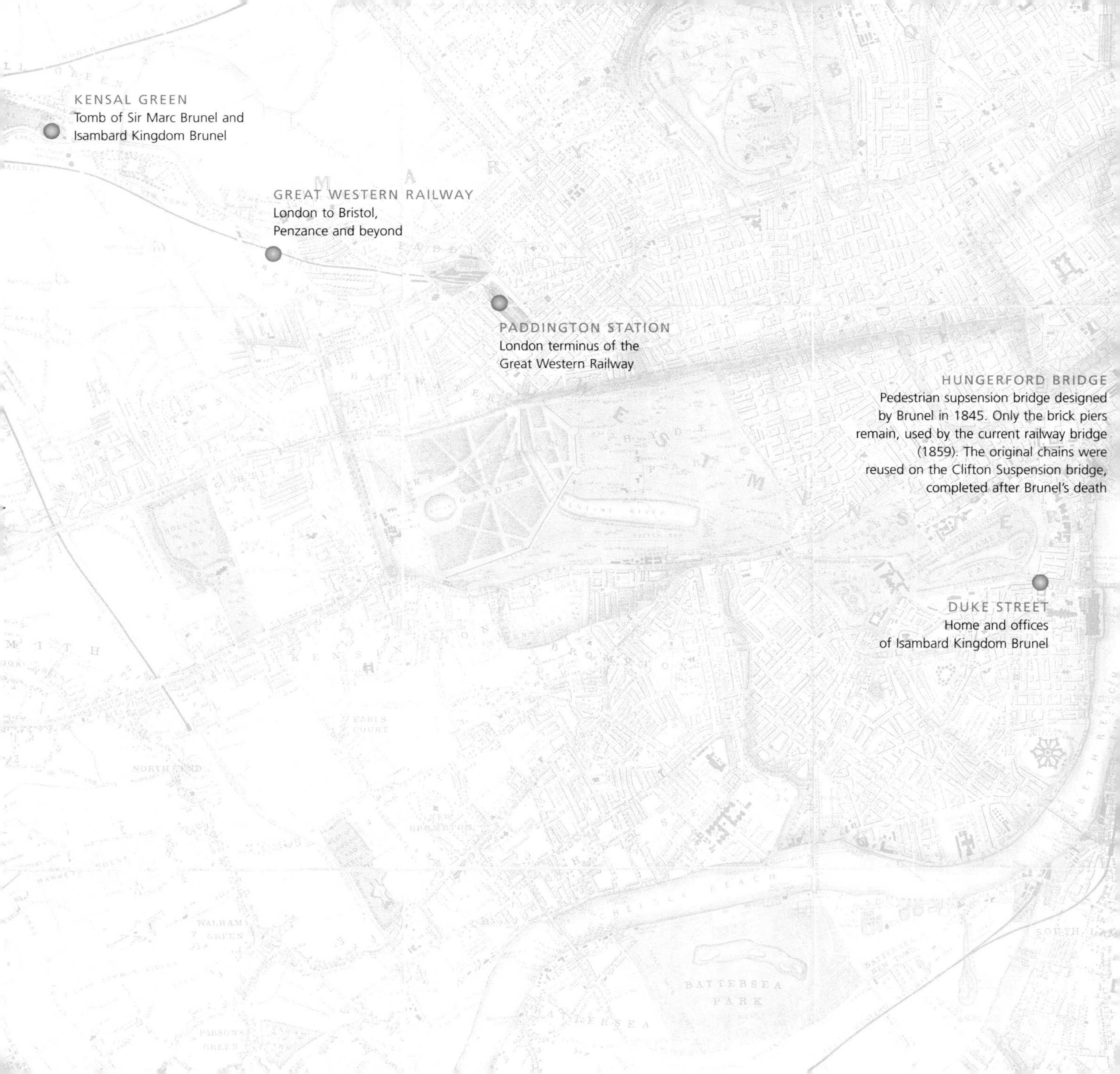
KENSAL GREEN
Tomb of Sir Marc Brunel and
Isambard Kingdom Brunel
GREAT WESTERN RAILWAY
London to Bristol,
Penzance and beyond
PADDINGTON STATION
London terminus of the
Great Western Railway
HUNGERFORD BRIDGE
Pedestrian supsension bridge designed
by Brunel in 1845. Only the brick piers
remain, used by the current railway bridge
(1859). The original chains were
reused on the Clifton Suspension bridge,
completed after Brunel's death
DUKE STREET
Home and offices
of Isambard Kingdom Brunel

Brunel's London

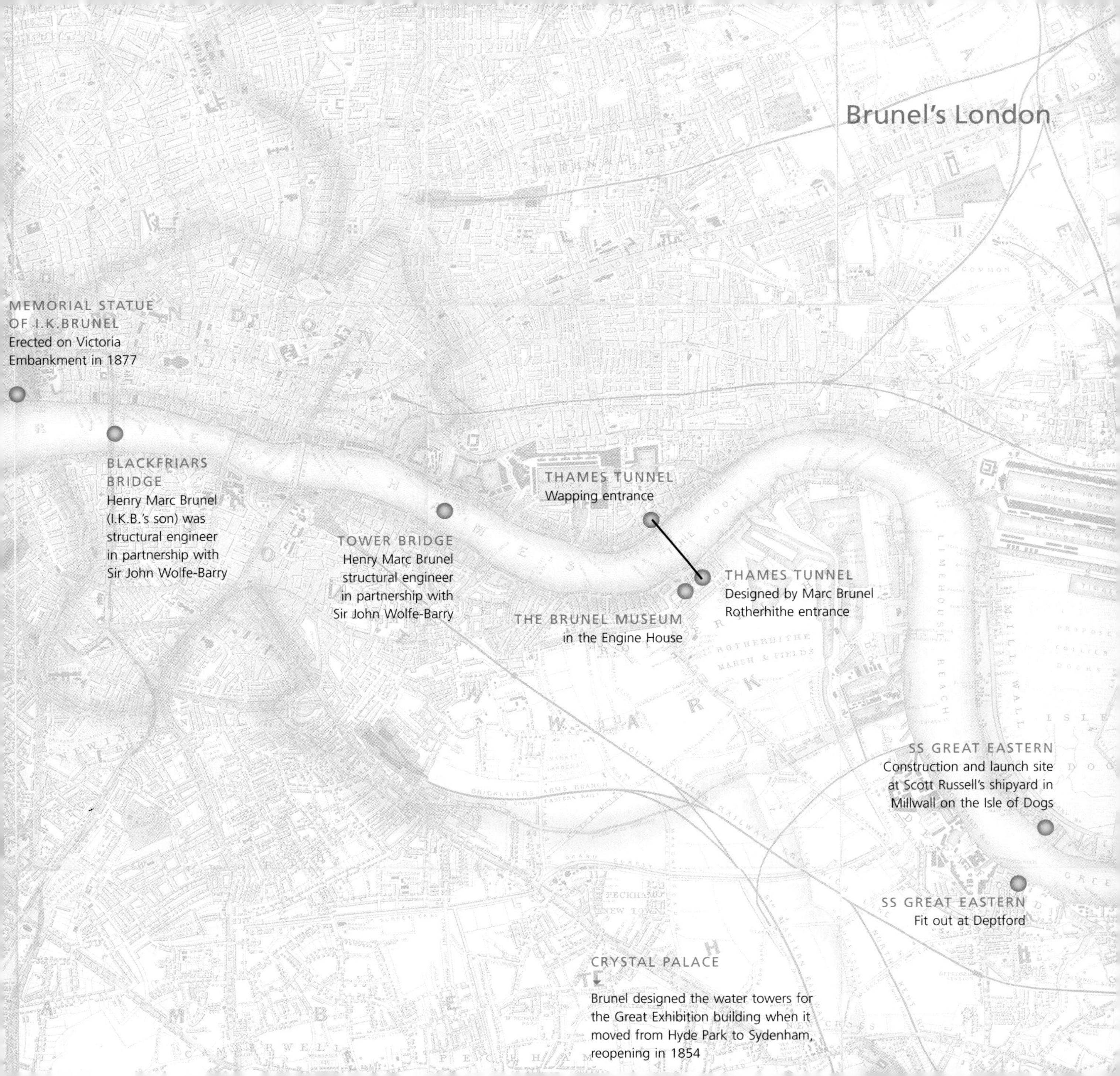

MEMORIAL STATUE OF I.K.BRUNEL
Erected on Victoria Embankment in 1877

BLACKFRIARS BRIDGE
Henry Marc Brunel (I.K.B.'s son) was structural engineer in partnership with Sir John Wolfe-Barry

TOWER BRIDGE
Henry Marc Brunel structural engineer in partnership with Sir John Wolfe-Barry

THAMES TUNNEL
Wapping entrance

THAMES TUNNEL
Designed by Marc Brunel
Rotherhithe entrance

THE BRUNEL MUSEUM
in the Engine House

SS GREAT EASTERN
Construction and launch site at Scott Russell's shipyard in Millwall on the Isle of Dogs

SS GREAT EASTERN
Fit out at Deptford

CRYSTAL PALACE
↓
Brunel designed the water towers for the Great Exhibition building when it moved from Hyde Park to Sydenham, reopening in 1854

Introduction

In 2002 the BBC ran a series of programmes called 'Great Britons' in which the public were invited to vote for which individual was the most important in the nation's history. 'Greater' than Shakespeare, Darwin and Newton was the nineteenth-century engineer, Isambard Kingdom Brunel. He was second only to Sir Winston Churchill, Britain's prime minister during the Second World War.

Brunel's reputation as the best engineer Britain has ever produced remains undiminished and unrivalled. His image - usually top hatted, smoking a cigar and leaning against massive chains (which were used to launch the *Great Eastern*) - is regularly deployed as an emblem of entrepreneurial engineering at its most flamboyant and imaginative.

More than any other, the city of Bristol has claimed Brunel as an adopted son. It is here that his steamship *Great Britain* has returned to the Great Western Dockyard where she had been built in 1843. Bristol is the 'country' terminus of his greatest railway project, the Great Western Railway (even if his original station is now a car park, but for how long?); and the spectacular Clifton Suspension Bridge (completed as a tribute to Brunel after this death) has been adopted as the emblem of the city.

But Brunel, born in Portsmouth, lived almost all his life in London. His design office was at 22 Duke Street in Westminster and there are more relics of his work throughout the capital than anywhere else in the country. They range from the minor – a street name in Kensington commemorating an observatory and the footprint of the water towers in Sydenham's Crystal Palace – to the major – Paddington Station, used by over 15 million commuters a year. A statue of Brunel by John Doubleday cast in 1982, sits between Platforms 8 and 9 (having been displaced in the 1990s refurbishment of the station from a more central position by the famous Peruvian, Paddington Bear).

Outside another London station, Charing Cross, the railway tracks cross the River Thames over what has been described as one of the ugliest bridges ever built, Hungerford Railway Bridge. It was, of course, not one of Brunel's. The designer was Sir John Hawkshaw and it opened five years after Brunel's death. But if you look carefully you will see two incongruous brick structures, one on each side of the river, standing a few yards into the water. These are the remains of an earlier Hungerford Bridge, a suspension footbridge designed by Brunel and completed in 1845. (When it closed to make way for the railway bridge, the suspension chains were taken to Bristol and recycled onto the Clifton Suspension Bridge, the completion of which was undertaken by the same Sir John Hawkshaw. Both Clifton and the new Hungerford Bridge opened in 1864).

If you take a ferry from Charing Cross Pier down the River Thames towards Greenwich, you will pass a bronze statue of Brunel cast by the sculptor Baron Carlo Marochetti in 1877, with a pedestal and surround by Norman Shaw on the Victoria Embankment, and a couple of miles downstream you will encounter another Brunel project. This one is almost invisible: it is the Thames Tunnel, linking Rotherhithe on the south bank with Wapping on the north.

The tunnel is now part of the London Overground and few commuters realise this is one of the most historically significant engineering sites in the world. It was here that successful underwater tunnelling began, with a boring technique that is still, using its basic principle, employed to this day. The scheme was devised by Isambard's father, Marc Brunel, with his son acting as his resident engineer.

There is one more site associated with Brunel on the Thames. As the river bends round the Isle of Dogs it passes a few timbers, gradually being eroded by every tide. These are the remains of the launch site of the *Great Eastern*, Brunel's last and most ambitious project. It created a ship that would not be surpassed in length or tonnage for more than 40 years. In some respects it was Brunel's greatest failure, but in others it was his most far-sighted triumph.

This is the story of that remarkable vessel.

The *Great Eastern*

The great engineer

Isambard Kingdom Brunel was born on 9th April 1806 in a terraced house in Britain Street in the old part of Portsmouth, a short walk from the naval dockyard. Isambard's father Marc Isambard Brunel was a gifted mechanical engineer, a French royalist who had escaped the terrors of the Revolution by fleeing to America, forced to leave his English sweetheart, Sophia Kingdom, behind. He moved to England in 1799 partly to be reunited with her, but perhaps more importantly to help the British war effort against Napoleon. The Royal Navy was building more ships than ever before, but they needed blocks – the pulleys that raised and controlled yards and sails – in greater quantities than the dockyards' craftsmen could carve them. Marc revolutionised the process of block making by inventing a number of machines that completely mechanised their production. The Block House and the machines still survive in Portsmouth Dockyard, as overlooked as the story of the brilliant father of the great engineer.

A year after Isambard's birth, with Marc's work on the block-making machinery completed, the family moved to London, to Chelsea, in search of more opportunities for Marc's inventive genius. Isambard was educated locally at first, then at Hove, and finally at the Collège Henri Quatre in Paris (where he also worked for a while with the watchmaker Abraham Louis Breguet). Returning home as a 16-year old in August 1822, Isambard then became involved in all his father's projects, helping devise machinery for everything from veneer cutting to shoe making.

Not all their projects were a success (and none a great financial success): Marc experimented with steam boats on the Thames but it led nowhere; father and son spent many

Sir Marc Isambard Brunel by James Northcote, painted in 1812-13. In the background is one the working machine models Marc commissioned to demonstrate his method of industrialising the making of ships' blocks. The model is now in the collection of the National Maritime Museum.

years trying to develop a liquefied gas 'differential power engine', based on the decomposition of chloral hydrate which they hoped would one day replace steam, but they failed to make it work. However, they did have one outstanding success that revolutionised civil engineering: they built the world's first sub-riverine tunnel. Many attempts had been made to tunnel under rivers such as the Thames, using the techniques of mining. Marc devised the system of a tunnelling shield followed by a team of bricklayers to immediately consolidate the excavation. The Thames Tunnel Company formed in 1824 and Isambard was formally appointed its resident engineer on 3rd January 1827. However, the project was bedevilled by flooding (and was not completed until 1843) and in one, in January 1828, Isambard was nearly drowned. He was lucky to survive – six of the workers in the tunnel did not.

Isambard was still recuperating from his accident in 1829 when he heard of a competition for the design of a bridge to span the Avon at Clifton. He had worked with his father on several bridge designs, including unsuccessful tenders for Kingston, Île de Bourbon and the Serpentine and his competition entry showed many similarities to these (although Marc had suggested a solution for Clifton that included a central pier). Thirteen submissions were received but one of Isambard's designs was eventually chosen as the winner, even over a late entry from the eminent Thomas Telford. Ironically, lack of funds meant that the bridge was not completed in his lifetime, nor quite to the design he proposed, but the Clifton Suspension Bridge was the project that launched Isambard as an engineer in his own right.

Isambard would go on to design 130 bridges, numberless tunnels, dry docks, stations, piers and hundreds of miles of railway lines. Of the lines he was responsible for, the Great Western Railway, with its broad gauge (too far ahead of its time), is perhaps the one he is most closely associated with. In 1835 he was at a meeting of the Great Western Railway's board when one of the directors queried the length of the line going all the way to Bristol. Brunel is said to have retorted: 'Why not make it longer and have a steamboat go from Bristol to New York and call it the Great Western?' From that comment, the Great Western Steamship Company was born and Brunel set about designing his first ship.

This was exactly the time when a new breed of fast emigrant ships were emerging – the clippers. Steam engines in ships were thought of as suitable only

Paddle steamer Great Western *in a gale*, by Samuel Walters

for short runs, or as a secondary means of propelling a ship when there was no wind. But Brunel could see that future lay in steam, not sail.

His *Great Western* was a wooden ship, built as strongly as a naval vessel. Propelled by paddle wheels, when she was completed in 1838 she was the largest steamship in the world with the largest marine engine ever built to power it. She did not, however, have the most promising of starts to her career. Steaming from London, where her engines had been installed, back to Bristol, a fire broke out in the engine room. Brunel, on his way to investigate, stepped on a burnt out ladder rung and fell 20 feet, badly injuring himself. The fire caused many of those who planned to take the maiden voyage across the Atlantic to cancel: when the ship got underway seven days later, there were only seven passengers on board. Nevertheless, she made the crossing in 17 days, only narrowly failing (by a few hours) to be the first steamship to cross the Atlantic from England to New York. Her rival, the *Sirius* had set off four days earlier. Returning to England, *Sirius* took 18 days to make the passage; the *Great Western* took 14.

So successful was this demonstration of the reliability, speed and predictability of his ship, that the fire was quickly forgotten and Brunel and the company began to plan their next vessel. This was the *Great Britain* and she was to be a vessel quite unlike the *Great Western*. The new ship would not be built of wood but of wrought iron. Wooden ships required massive frames and beams for strength: iron frames took up much less space, leaving much more room for cargo. She would not have paddle engines; she would have a screw propeller. This method of propulsion had only just been invented and characteristically Brunel grasped its significance ahead of most engineers. The six-bladed propeller he designed for the *Great Britain* was only marginally less efficient than the propellers of today. Ready for sea trials in 1845, the *Great Britain* was the largest ship afloat and she would be the first iron ocean-going vessel, and the first vessel with a propeller to cross the Atlantic.

But ships were only a small part of Brunel's output. He continued to work on railways, bridges and tunnels. After the launch of the *Great Britain*, he was mainly occupied with the Cornwall and East Cornwall railways. This involved designing numerous wooden bridges, but also designing and supervising the building of an enormous iron bridge linking Devon and Cornwall over the River Tamar at Saltash.

An engraving of the *Great Britain* in a gale, after a painting by J. Walter

The *Great Eastern*'s builder John Scott Russell, with plans of the ship in his hands and a framed picture of her on the wall

Brunel was also very active in the organisation of the Great Exhibition of 1851, the famous celebration of design, industry and manufacture. He was chairman of the Jury for Civil Engineering, Architecture and Building Contrivances and a member of the jury on the machinery section. In addition, he served on the Building Committee, even collaborating with his fellow members to design a building to house the exhibition. However, when Joseph Paxton submitted his proposal for a 'crystal palace' Brunel immediately became an active supporter of his 'greenhouse' design. In the grand opening procession on 1st May 1851, Brunel proudly walked fourth from the front.

He could not have known that within days he would start the preparatory work for the greatest ship of all, a project on which he would work for the rest of his life.

The shipbuilder

Another engineer involved in the organisation of Great Exhibition was the naval architect and shipbuilder John Scott Russell, who was to be the builder of the *Great Eastern*. Two years older than Brunel, Russell's career looked at the outset as if it would follow an academic path, but by the early 1830s it had taken a more practical turn as he began designing and building steam road carriages. He was then commissioned to look into improving the speed of canal boats, which at that time were mostly still pulled by horses. This led him to develop an explanation of the effect produced by moving a boat though a restricted body of water – the Wave of Translation or the Solitary Wave. Although this phenomenon had been observed before Russell's experiments, he was the first to be able to explain it by theory, and, crucially, he was able to demonstrate the relationship between the speed of the wave and the depth of water. It was clear to him that if a boat could catch and ride the Wave of Translation, it could be pulled more quickly.

Much pioneering work had been done earlier in the century in both iron boat building and marine steam engines in the canals around Glasgow, and it was here that Russell built a number of experimental canal boats in iron to develop the lines of least resistance. His canal boats were unique: for the first time vessels were build not to mimic the techniques of wooden shipbuilding, but to exploit iron for its structural strength. Their design included bulkheads and longitudinal framing: not features of wooden vessels.

Russell was convinced that his wave line theory could also be applied to sea-going vessels, and hull shapes could be developed that pushed the water aside with the least resistance. One of his recommendations was for hollow (concave) waterlines at the bow, based on a sine curve. Although the theory was eventually proved not to be entirely correct, all subsequent naval architecture has confirmed that fine-lined ships are the best hydrodynamic form.

In 1838 Russell took on a managerial role at Caird's Greenock shipyard in 1838 and built a succession of steamships designed in accordance with his wave line theory. In 1844 he moved to London and quickly established himself within the scientific community. The following year he became secretary of the Royal Society of Arts. He would have known Brunel through both the Institution of Civil Engineers and the organising of the Great Exhibition.

In partnership with the three Robinson brothers, Henry, Alfred and Richard, Russell took over William Fairburn's shipyard on London's Isle of Dogs, almost opposite the Royal Navy yard at Deptford. Fairburn had abandoned the yard as uneconomic and had returned to his native Scotland but the new owners were more successful. They built a series of unique vessels, including Robert Stephenson's schooner yacht *Titania* in 1850 (although it was the defeat of this yacht (and others) in a race around the Isle of Wight the following year by the *America* that led to the America's Cup competition). By 1851 Russell had become the sole owner of the yard on the Isle of Dogs, and, thanks to a recommendation from Brunel, had two steamers for the Australian Mail Steam Company on the books. He also built a second *Titania* for Stephenson in 1853, with a bow remarkably similar, if in miniature, to that of the big ship he was about to embark on.

May 1851: Brunel's opinion is sought by The Australian Mail Steam Company

In the same month that the Great Exhibition opened, the Australian Mail Steam Company approached Brunel for advice on the optimal steamship for Australia. He calculated the appropriate dimensions – 5,000 to 6,000 tons, because such a vessel would have the capacity to carry enough coal to need only one stop to refuel on the way to Australia. The Company, presumably feeling that these would be exceptionally large vessels (the *Great Britain* was after all only 3,600 tons), did not take his advice, although they did commission two vessels, *Adelaide* and *Victoria*, of less than 2,000 tons from John Scott Russell.

A page from one of Brunel's sketchbooks, dated August 1853. It includes sketches of a sailing warship, suggesting that he was thinking about how much the *Great Eastern* might heel in strong winds and how much sail she should carry. The vessel would carry far more than indicated here.

However, Brunel continued to mull the question the Company had posed for the rest of the year, and into the next. Perhaps even 6,000 tons was not the optimal size of a ship for Australia. Perhaps the ship should be big enough to carry all the coal she needed to reach Australia and return without refuelling at all. She could be laden with the finest Welsh coal, not the inferior stuff the coaling stations sold, and shave significant time off the voyage by never stopping on the way to her destination.

March 1852: Brunel draws the first sketch of a giant ship with paddle wheels and a screw propeller

On 25th March 1852 he wrote in his sketchbook 'East India Steamship' and beneath he scribbled 'Say 600 feet x 65 feet x 30 feet'. This was an extraordinary leap of imagination: the largest ship of the time, the Cunard Line's *Persia*, was 398 feet in length. A promenade around the deck of such a ship as Brunel was contemplating would be a walk of more than a quarter of a mile. In fact, when the design was finalised the ship was nearly 700 ft long and six times larger in tonnage than the *Great Britain*. The dimensions were developed in his sketchbook into drawings of a steamship that looked like nothing ever built, a leviathan with five funnels and six masts.

Initially Brunel thought of sheathing the iron hull in wood, and then sheathing this with copper plates to stop barnacles, molluscs and weed attaching to the hull and slowing the ship down. At this time anti-fouling for iron ships was still relatively poor in comparison, but nevertheless he eventually opted for a completely iron hull. From his experience in designing the *Great Britain* Brunel knew that a screw propeller would be more energy efficient than paddle engines. But he realised that manoeuvrability would be an issue for such a large vessel, so he designed this ship with paddle engines as well.

The draft of the ship was determined by the depth of water in the River Hoogly at Calcutta. The river had a navigable depth of 24ft; Brunel calculated a draft of 23ft when the ship had burnt half her coal getting there at an average speed of 15 knots (18 miles an hour).

In common with all merchant ships of the period, she was designed to carry masts and 6,500 square yards of sails too (the clipper *Cutty Sark*, launched in 1869, carried 3,600 square yards of canvas). However, unlike any other ship, she had six

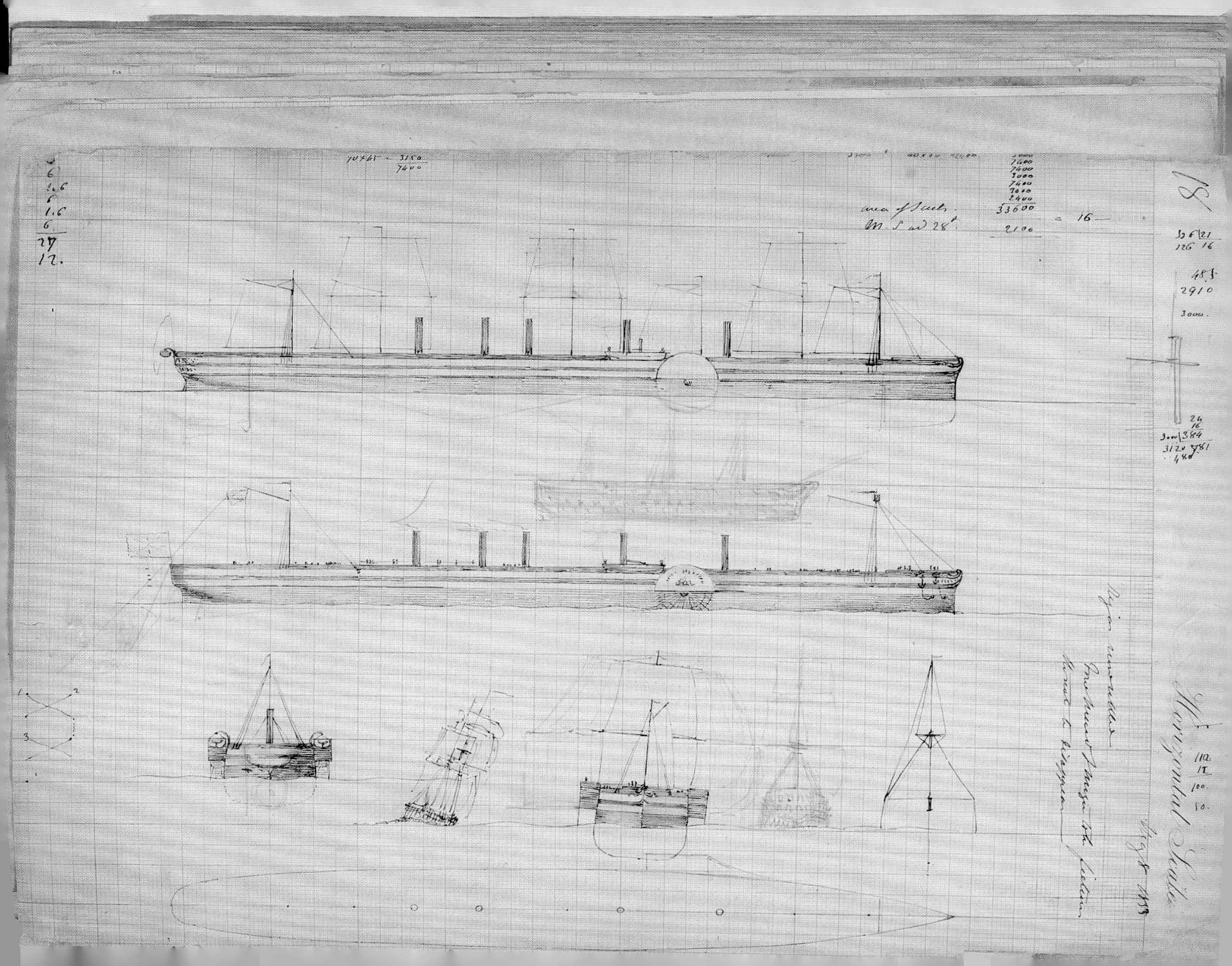

masts, named, with a complete disregard for maritime convention, after the days of the week (there was no Sunday mast: perhaps relating to the old sailors' joke of there being no day of rest at sea).

The hull was designed to be immensely strong. It had to be: if the bow and stern were lifted by different waves, the middle of the ship had to rigid enough not to sag. She was double-bottomed: effectively there was one hull inside another, 2 feet 10 inches apart. Ten transverse watertight bulkheads divided the ship into 60ft compartments, while two longitudinal bulkheads, 36ft apart, ran the entire length of the ship, right through the engine and boiler rooms and extending up to the ship's load line. Underneath the teak planks of the main deck was another cellular iron structure: remarkably similar in concept to the Britannia Bridge across the Menai Strait, recently designed by Brunel's friend Robert Stephenson.

She was flat-bottomed for the simple reason that no dry dock in the world could accommodate her: when the time came for maintenance she had to be able to sit upright on a huge gridiron in a tidal river estuary.

Going against the common preference for a sheerline (the top edge of the vessel) that sweeps up from the middle of the ship to the bow, and less steeply towards the stern, which also gives a reserve of buoyancy, Brunel dispensed with any curve at all. The sheerline was perfectly horizontal. It gave the ship an unorthodox look, but it made construction simpler.

The ship would accommodate 4,000 passengers – 800 first class, 2,000 second class and 1,200 third class with a crew of about 400. The cabins and public rooms would be located in the centre of the ship, where movement of the ship would be felt the least as she rode through the waves, and insulated from the noise and vibrations of the engines by coal bunkers.

July 1852: Brunel's proposal for the great ship is accepted by the Eastern Steam Navigation Company

In January 1851 the Eastern Steam Navigation Company had been formed with the intention of establishing a shipping line from Britain to India, China and Australia. Key to their business plan was securing the mail contract from the British government. They tendered for it, but in March 1852 the Government decided to award the contract to the Peninsular & Oriental Steam Navigation Company instead. So the Eastern Steam Navigation Company became a company without a purpose. However, it was at this precise moment that Brunel finalised his concept for the big ship. Having discussed it with a number of colleagues, including John Scott Russell, he submitted a paper to the Eastern Steam Navigation Company. He treated the challenge of building a vessel six times larger than anything else afloat lightly: 'Nothing more novel is proposed now, but again to build a vessel of the size required to carry her own coals for the voyage... Size in a ship is an element of speed, and of strength, and of safety, and of great relative economy, instead of a disadvantage; and it is limited only by the extent of demand for freight, and by the circumstances of the ports frequented.'

The board of the Eastern Steam Navigation Company invited Brunel to present his ideas. Unable to attend he asked Russell to represent him. The upshot was that in July 1852, Brunel was appointed as Engineer to the Company and was authorised to seek tenders for the building of the great ship.

December 1853: the contracts for constructing the hull and engines are let

Tenders were organised and the winning bidder for both the hull and the paddle engines was John Scott Russell. The contract for the screw engines was awarded to James Watt & Co.

Although the *Great Eastern* was a ship of Brunel's – and affectionately called by him the 'Great Babe' – she is also the greatest achievement of the builder, John Scott Russell. At a dinner to celebrate the completion of her fit-out on 8th August 1859 (at which Brunel was absent), Russell told the guests that:

> 'It was part of an original understanding between Mr. Brunel and himself that they should never interfere with each other in the duty to which they might be specially called. It was part of his understanding with him, that the original conception of a large steam-ship to carry her own coal upon the longest voyage, so as to avoid all the waste of time and expense which was then standing in the way of steam navigation for long distances, was absolutely and entirely Mr. Brunel's and not his in the smallest degree. It was quite true that very soon after the thought struck Mr. Brunel he came to him, and said, "Now, I am not a ship-builder, nor am I an engine-builder, and I now come to you to see if you will devote your mind and attention to the

Hand-coloured lithographs of the *Great Eastern* presented to the Patent Museum (the predecessor of the Science Museum) by John Scott Russell in 1861. The underlying drawings are same as those (uncoloured) in his *The Modern System of Naval Architecture* published in 1864.

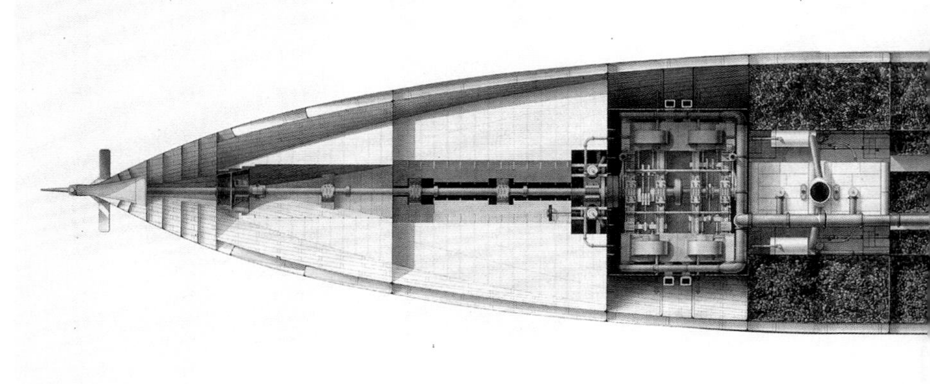

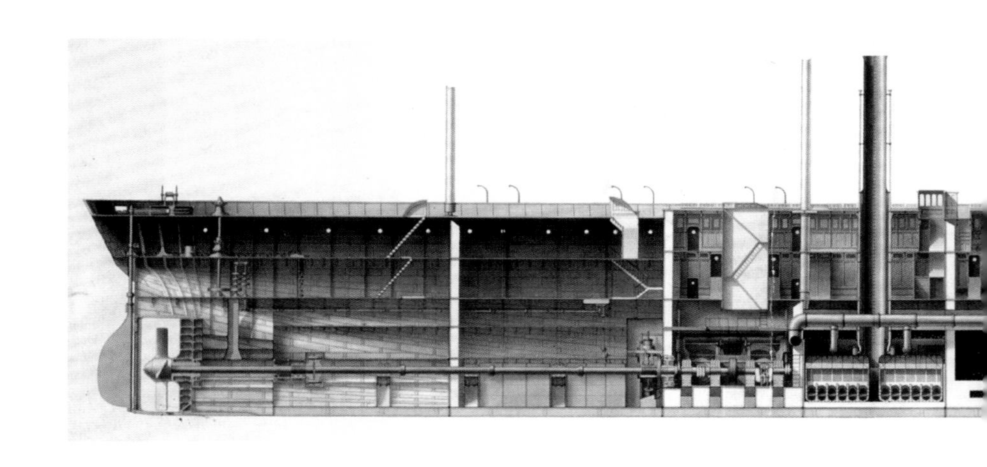

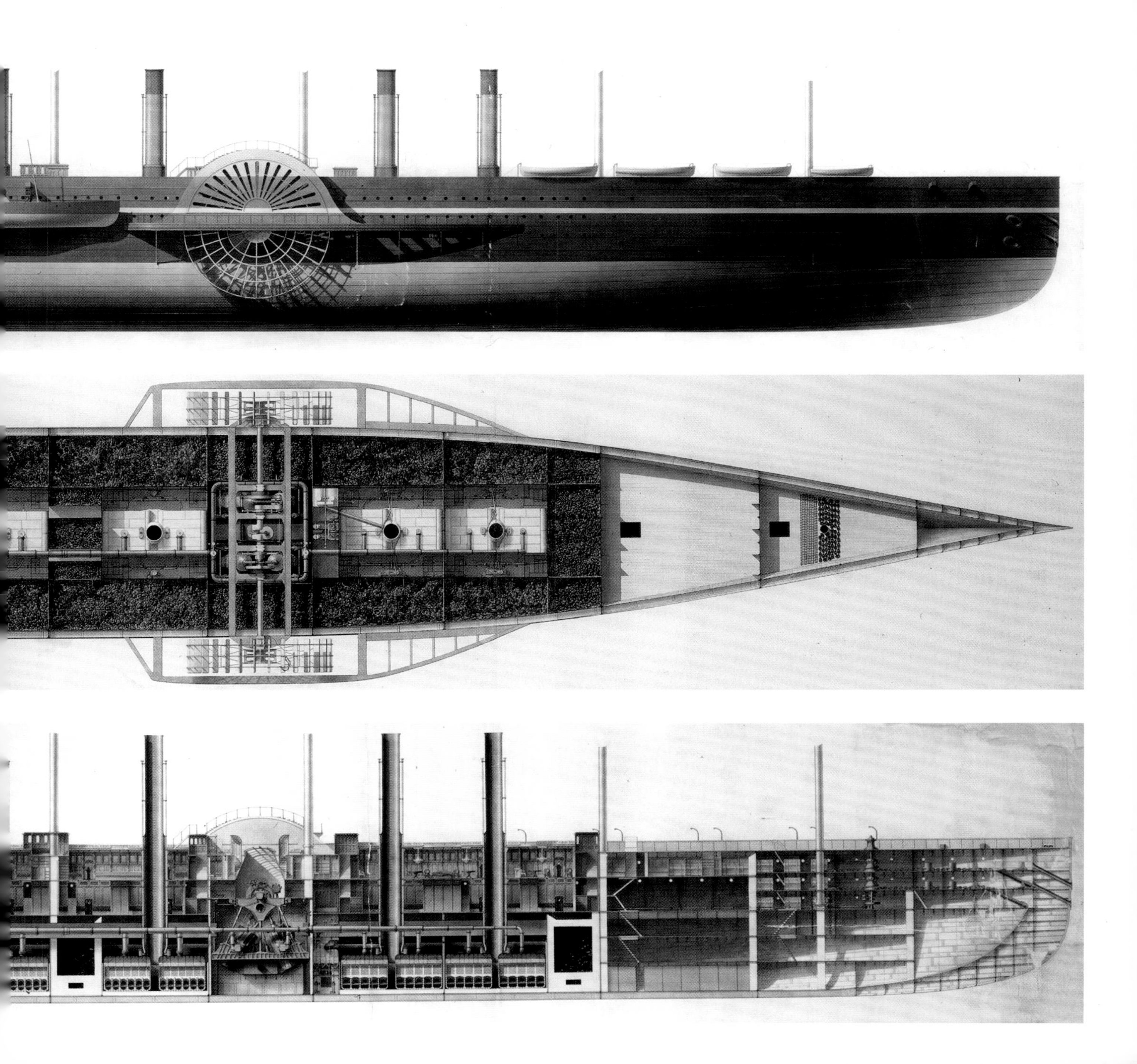

The launch site at Burrell's Wharf in 2016

> carrying out of this problem to a successful issue. You and I will go together through the whole undertaking pari passu ['on an equal footing'], you shall design the ship according to your own lines, make the engines upon your own plan, and construct the ship according to the best of your experience and knowledge, but we shall always agree on this– that I am the father of the undertaking, and that I had the original conception." In this he agreed, and to this he was happy now to bear testimony, for nothing had tended more to his unhappiness than upon many occasions to have received compliments for the invention, or original idea, when he could assure the company [at the dinner] that he was totally innocent of it. His responsibility was the construction, as a naval architect, of the lines of the ship. If the ship was slow, if she had bad qualities, the responsibility was his alone–- if in regard to her structure she was ill made, ill planned – if her materials were ill disposed or ill put together, that was his fault, and if her engines did not, her paddle engines especially, work well – if her boilers were not equal to their work, then he was almost entirely the only man to blame."

Brunel had estimated the cost of the ship at £500,000. Russell's tender for the ship was £275,000 with the paddle wheels costing an additional £44,000 with the screw engines costing another £60,000. This would have left £121,000 for the launch and the fit-out of the vessel. Brunel, a man hugely experienced in contracts and estimates, was satisfied. Shareholders would also have been encouraged by the new Chairman of the Eastern Steam Navigation Company – Charles Geach, Member of Parliament for Coventry and iron magnate. Geach was also a director of Beale & Company, which would supply the iron plates for the ship's hull.

The contract given to Russell from which the detailed design was to be developed was not overly prescriptive. It specified, for example, that 'All vertical joints to be butt joints and to be double riveted wherever required by the engineer... No cast iron to be used anywhere except for slide valves and cocks without special permission of the engineer. The water-tightness of every part to be tested before launching, and several compartments to be filled [with water] one at a time up to the level of the lower deck.' However, every detailed design drawing Russell produced was rigorously scrutinised by Brunel and commented upon. For example, in February 1854 Brunel wrote in his memorandum book:

> 'It is evident that large weights may most easily be wasted or saved by a careless or close consideration. I found, for instance, an unnecessary introduction of a filling strip, such as is frequently used in ship-building to avoid bending to angle-irons; made a slight alteration in the disposition of the plates that rendered this unnecessary; found that we had saved 40 tons in weight of iron, or say £1,200 of money in first cost, and 40 tons of cargo freight – at least £3,000 a year. The principle of construction of the ship is, in fact, entirely new if merely from the rule I have laid down, and shall rigidly preserve, and in the direction and in the proportion, in which it is required and can be usefully employed for the strength of the ship, and none merely for the purpose of facilitating the framing and first construction. In the present construction of iron ships the plates are not proportioned to the strength required at different parts, and nearly twenty per cent of the weight is expended in angle-irons or frames, which may be useful or convenient in the mere putting together of the whole as great box, but is almost useless, or very much misapplied, in affecting the strength of the structure as a ship. All this misconstruction I forbid, and the consequence is that every part has to be considered and designed as if an iron ship had never before been built; indeed I believe we should get on much quicker if we had no previous habits and prejudices on the subject.

The site of the *Great Eastern*'s construction: the ship and launchways superimposed on a 2016 aerial photograph

Neither Brunel nor Russell were traditional shipbuilders: both were men prepared to take a radical new approach.

February 1854: construction begins

An approved design was ready by the beginning of 1854, and construction could begin. First, a thousand wooden piles, each thirty feet long, were driven into the ground. On the tops of these timber baulks were laid and this was the structure on which the enormous ship was built.

Early in the construction, the lower section of a bulkhead is being fitted to an iron girder that will form part of the ship's keel. Photograph by Joseph Cundall, April 1855.

The hull was built up of 30,000 wrought iron plates, weighing an average of 1/3rd of a ton. The lower ones were an inch thick, the upper ones ¾ inch. Each had to be lifted into place by either hand tackles or the great steam crane that stretched across the hull, then secured to its neighbours by a hundred rivets. For three and a half years, 400 hammers worked 12 hours a day for six days a week to drive in the three million rivets needed. Given the scale of the enterprise, casualties were surprisingly light. One worker fell to his death, another fell on a co-worker and killed him; a boy fell and was impaled on a standing iron bar, and a visitor bent over the head of a pile when the monkey (the iron block of a pile driver) came down and crushed his skull. However, no evidence has ever been found for the widely and persistently believed story that a riveter had been trapped between the inner and outer hulls.

In Birmingham James Watt & Co. was building the screw engines, while on the Isle of Dogs Russell was building the paddle engines. This was not something he could accomplish alone. The paddle shafts were made by Fulton & Neilson at the Lancefield Forge in Glasgow, where special furnaces had to be constructed because the shafts were so much larger than anything the company had made before. Even so, there were two failures before the 40-ton forgings were perfect.

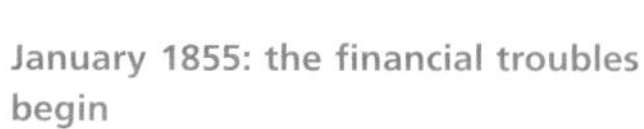

January 1855: the financial troubles begin

Less than a year into construction, on New Year's Day 1855, Russell told Brunel he was in financial difficulties and his credit had been stopped. Brunel persuaded the Eastern Steam Navigation Company's board to agree to ease Russell's cash flow by paying for the work done in instalments of £8,000. But Russell then had a run of bad luck. The

Crimean War (1853-56) created a massive demand for ships, pushing up the cost of wages and materials hugely. Not only that, the ironclad battery H.M.S. *Aetna* Russell was building in the same yard caught fire on 3rd May 1855, revealing that the yard was underinsured. Not only that, the Eastern Steam Navigation Company's chairman Charles Geach, who might have given him favourable terms for paying for the iron plates, had died in November of the previous year.

In early October Russell informed Brunel that his bank was demanding a repayment of £12,000 against an overdraft of £15,000. Brunel offered £10,000 – the bank responded by demanding the full £15,000. But Russell needed the money to pay his men otherwise he would have to lay them off, although many of them were not working on the big ship but on six others he was building at the same time (Russell built at least ten vessels during the construction of the *Great Eastern*).

Brunel was clearly frustrated with his shipbuilder: in the same month he wrote to Russell: 'How the devil can you say you satisfied yourself of the weight of the ship when the figures your Clerk gave you are 1,000 tons less than I make it or than you made it a few months ago. For *shame*, if you are satisfied. I am sorry to give you trouble but I think you will thank me for it. I wish you were my obedient servant, I should begin by a little flogging.'

The situation lurched on, yet the Company felt confident enough to appoint William Harrison as the ship's captain, with responsibility for the navigation and accommodation arrangements. But in February 1856 Brunel, fearing that Russell's creditors might seize the ship, advised the Eastern Steam Navigation Company to take possession of the ship, on the grounds of breach of contract.

To this day, arguments rage about whether Brunel forced Russell into insolvency or Russell massively mismanaged the finances of the project. Either way, once the ship was seized by the Company, the bank refused to honour Russell's cheques and he had no choice but to dismiss all his workmen.

Russell was bankrupt. He repudiated his contract with the Eastern Steam Navigation Company, handing the ship over to them. He had received £292,295 (which included extra work the company had commissioned) but only a quarter of the work on the hull had been completed. And 1,200 tons of iron supplied for the ship had not been used on her but diverted to the other ships in Russell's yard. Brunel now took personal control of the project.

The construction *on* August 21st 1855. The photograph by Joseph Cundall shows the cellular construction of the ship, with the hull divided by bulkheads reaching up to the top deck. If, 57 years later, the *Titanic*'s bulkheads had compartmentalised the ship so completely, she would not have sunk.

OVERLEAF
By May 1856 the plating of the ship was substantially complete

Just before the launch began, the daughter of the Great Eastern Steam Navigation Company's chairman broke a garlanded bottle of champagne against the ship's bow and bade "God speed the *Leviathan*!"

The bow of the *Great Eastern*, 2nd November 1857, the day before the first attempt to launch the ship. Photograph by Robert Howlett.

May 1856:
construction recommences

The Company was to be a shipbuilder for three times longer than it planned, yet the press accounts of the time, at least until the time when the ship was launched, were more intent on celebrating the enormity of the feat than criticising the management of the construction. The ship was a source of immense pride for patriotic Victorians. The biggest ship, conceived by the greatest engineer, was being built in the world's biggest and greatest capital. And it did not escape notice that, although the ship was planned to be a merchant vessel, ten thousand troops could be embarked on her and despatched to anywhere on the globe should the need arise. There was even speculation that, had she been available, the Indian Mutiny of 1857-58 might have been suppressed more rapidly or more thoroughly.

Not only the press was excited by the ship: a whole industry sprang up producing pottery and lithographic souvenirs, while music publishers turned out, it could be said by the score, polkas, gallops and marches. And the shipyard on the Isle of Dogs itself became one of the world's great tourist attractions: visitors could take a steamer from one of the central London piers – such as Hungerford (beside Brunel's suspension bridge), or beside the tunnel his father had built -- which travelled every twenty minutes towards Greenwich for 6d. or 4d. Or they could take the Blackwall Railway to Limehouse where an omnibus ran every half hour to the shipyard. The price of admission was 2s. 6d. However, visiting times were limited – between from one to half-past one on weekdays (after which a bell would ring and the workmen, having had their dinner, would return) and from half-past three to half-past four on Saturdays.

November 1857- January 1858: the launch

The contract for the ship signed by Russell on 22nd November 1853 stipulated that the ship was to be built in a dock. However, this was dismissed by both Russell and Brunel very early on in the project as too expensive. A traditional slipway launch, with the vessel gliding down a slipway stern first, was not feasible for practical reasons: the Thames was not wide or deep enough. Furthermore the slipway would have to be built with an inclined plane of around 1 in 14, and for a ship the size of the *Great Eastern* this would have meant the bow of the ship was

Laying the teak planks of the main deck, 11th February 1857, photographed by Robert Howlett

100 ft above ground. A sideways launch was the only option. Russell favoured a free launch down greased wooden launch ways, but Brunel feared the timber cradles would bind on the timber launch ways. He also wanted the launch to be very tightly controlled.

Launching a ship sideways was not a new idea: it had been done for over a century, but of course no ship as large as this had ever been launched, and Brunel devised an elaborate system to give him the control he wanted. The ship was supported on two timber cradles, 120 feet wide and 110 feet apart (so the bow projected 180 ft beyond the forward cradle and the stern). On the underside of the cradles were iron bars, one inch thick, seven inches wide and eleven inches apart, laid parallel to the ship. From the cradles to the water (and beyond – the low water mark was 240 feet from the ship's starboard side; the launch-ways extended to 330 feet), the ground had been prepared with an inclination of 1 in 12 and covered with a layer of concrete two feet thick. Embedded in the concrete were one-foot square timbers, 2 ½ feet apart. Another layer of timbers were laid on top of these, two feet apart, and finally on top of these, 18 inches apart were iron rails (exactly the same as the broad gauge rails Brunel had designed for the

Great Western Railway line). These rails were at right angles to the ship, and formed the surface on which the bars under the cradles would slide. Or should have slid.

To each of the launching cradles a 2 5/8-inch chain, borrowed from the Admiralty, was attached, wound round huge checking drums to restrain the vessel from moving too quickly down the slipway, or to stop one end moving more quickly than the other. Rather than relying on gravity alone to move the ship down the launch ways, steam winches were set up to haul on chains which ran out to barges moored in the middle of the river and back to the bow and stern. There would of course be some initial friction as metal bit on metal, but Brunel had two hydraulic presses in place, each able to deliver 300 tons of pressure, to give an initial push.

The date of Tuesday 3rd November 1857 was set for the launch. Brunel announced: 'I propose to commence operations about two hours before high water and to endeavour to get the ship down as quickly as I can into the water and down to within about thirty-six feet of the bottom of the ways.' He wanted to get the ship clear of the cradles and have the ship floated by the high tide on the following afternoon. His orders were:

> 'Provided the mechanical arrangements should prove efficient, the success of the operation will depend entirely upon the perfect regularity and absence of haste or confusion in each stage of the proceeding and in every department and to attain this, nothing is more essential than perfect silence. I would earnestly request therefore that the most positive orders are given to the men not to speak a word and that every endeavour should be made to prevent a sound being heard, except the simple orders quietly and deliberately given by those few who will direct.'

The Times downplayed the event, stating: 'The launch is likely to be a long and tedious affair, which will probably occupy eight to ten hours.' However, the Eastern Steam Navigation Company, unknown to Brunel but seeing an opportunity to raise a little money, sold tickets to the public. One journalist estimated that 10,000 people were in the yard when he arrived in the early morning and by noon it was nearer 100,000. Grandstands had been built overnight outside the yard, and

One of the great checking drums, which were to prevent the ship sliding too quickly down the slipway, photographed by Robert Howlett. When the launch began, the handles flew up, killing three men.

hundreds of spectators also took to the water to see the spectacle of the world's largest ship enter the water.

Brunel spent half an hour clearing visitors away from the gear before he could take his place on the launching platform. It was not a good moment for the Eastern Steam Navigation Company's directors to give him a number of options for the ship's name. Brunel replied: 'Call her Tom Thumb if you like.'

At 12.30, the daughter of Henry Hope, the Company chairman, broke a bottle of champagne over the bow and christened the ship, not *Great Eastern*, but *Leviathan.* Brunel waved a white flag – the order to release the bow and stern fastenings and slacken the restraining chains. The stern began to move. Brunel now raised his red flag, ordering the hydraulic rams to start to push.

So awesome was the sight of this great ship moving that everyone stood still in wonder... including the gang on the stern checking drum. They were leaning on the drum's handles so when the stern cradle started to move quickly and the drum revolved rapidly, two of the men were thrown into the air. One was to die from his injuries. At the subsequent inquest Brunel took responsibility: 'I may blame myself, for I did not anticipate the handles would have revolved so quickly.' Meanwhile, some of the crewmen on the river barges, fearing that the ship was out of control, threw themselves into the Thames. Brunel now ordered the checking drums to be braked. The *Leviathan* had moved four feet towards the water.

By the time Brunel could organise the re-start of the launch, it was 2.00 p.m., and raining heavily. The attempt failed – the bow winch stripped its gears and chains snapped, and the ship remained unmoved, unmoveable. The day was over, some of the crowd re-christening the ship the *Leave-her-high-and-dry-athan*.

The next opportunity for launch would be the high tide on 19th November. This time Brunel managed to keep the yard closed to the public. He had borrowed another two hydraulic rams to push the ship, but as soon as they were applied, the timber abutments holding them gave way and no progress was made. The 28th of November was a more successful day: the rams got the ship moving at a rate of an inch a minute, but after the workmen returned from their dinner break, she was again stuck. The weight of the ship had forced the rails on the launch ways into the timbers supporting them so the cradles were now lying in small hollows. On top of that, mooring chains on two of the barges in the river broke. The launch attempt was halted yet again. The ship had moved 14 feet.

Nov 18,

PREVIOUS PAGE

The *Great Eastern* almost ready for launch on 12th November 1857. Only two of her funnels have been fitted, the others lie on the deck. Photograph by Robert Howlett.

The chains were repaired overnight and with the help of more borrowed equipment the ship moved another eight feet on 29th November. This was a Sunday, and working on this day brought the wrath of the Sabbatarians, but the journal *The Engineer* was more sympathetic spiritually: 'A brave man struggling with adversity was, according to the ancients, a spectacle the Gods loved to look down on.'

The 30th November improved on the previous day's performance by six inches before a jack failed. But by adding an extra two jacks to each cradle, the ship moved forward another 14 feet. There was still huge public interest in progress – a spectators' stage had been erected outside the yard and on this day it collapsed, causing around two hundred people to fall 20 feet to the ground. Seven of them were seriously injured, but none fatally.

Fourteen feet were again achieved on 3rd December, and on the 4th (before two rams failed) and again on the 5th. With the ship now 60 feet away from the ram abutments, new abutments had to be built. It was also the day of a visit from Victoria the Princess Royal (who the following year would marry the German emperor Frederick III). Among her party was a friend of Brunel's – Sir Joseph Paxton, the designer of the Crystal Palace.

Two days later, progress slowed to a total of eight feet. On the 16th December, the ship moved only three feet as parts of the equipment, rams and chains failed. But this was the day that Robert Stephenson arrived from his sick-bed to give his support and advice to his fellow engineer. As Brunel reported to the Eastern Steam Navigation Company Directors: 'After full consideration of all the circumstances and assisted by the best advice I could call to my aid, namely, that of my friend Mr Robert Stephenson, I considered that the only mode of proceeding, and one which there appeared no reason to doubt would succeed, was to apply considerably more press power; that I proposed to double what we had ...'

An order was sent to Richard Tangye's workshop in Birmingham – the same company that had supplied the 21-inch ram that Stephenson had used to lift the Britannia Bridge over the Menai Strait. It was a commission that would change the company's fortunes: as Tangye later declared: 'We launched the *Great Eastern* and the *Great Eastern* launched us.' The rams could now deliver a total force of 4,500 tons. Gravity contributed another 1,000 tons, so the combined force was nearly half the weight of the ship itself.

One of Tangye's hydraulic rams brought in to help push the ship into the water. The top-hatted figure may be Richard Tangye, the inventor, but this is not certain. Photograph by Robert Howlett.

Preparing for the launch, Brunel (second from the left) stands with his assistant William Jacomb (left) and the railway contractor Solomon Tredwell (right) whose company built the launchways. The man on the extreme left is sometime identified as the ship's captain William Harrison or John Scott Russell, but he resembles neither. Photograph by Robert Howlett.

Tangye's rams arrived in the New Year and now, instead of relying on barges alone, the haulage gear was fixed to the foreshore on the other side of the river, at Deptford. This was a fortunate precaution, as a barque running upstream on 4th January collided with one of the barges and sank it. Over the following two days the ship moved 20 feet and by 10th January, at high tide, she was partially afloat. From then on, she was gradually pushed further and further until the 14th when, with the forward cradle having travelled 197ft and the after cradle 207ft, Brunel called a halt to stop her being floated off on the high tide of the 19th – indeed water was pumped in to stop her launching herself. The day after this high tide had passed, the ship was finally in position for launch. This was now planned for 30th January.

When the day came, it was deemed too windy to have the monster ship in the water, so the launch was postponed to the following day – 31st January 1858. All night the water ballast was pumped out and at 1.30 p.m. the *Leviathan* was finally afloat. Four tugs – *Victoria* and the *Pride of All Nations* at the bow, *Napoleon* and *Perseverance* at the stern – guided the ship across the Thames to Deptford. But even this was not completely free of mishap: a barge managed to catch the starboard paddle wheel.

On 25th June 1858, the ship was registered, but as the *Great Eastern*: no mention was made in the document of *Leviathan*

February – August 1859: completion of the ship

The journey from drawing board to Deptford had cost £732,000 – nearly double the original estimate, but the ship was still far from ready to go to sea. The launch alone had cost £170,000 and the remaining works to make her into a functioning passenger ship would require another £172,000. The Eastern Steam Navigation Company was in serious trouble, so to prevent their creditors seizing the ship, a cunning plan was devised. They created a new firm, the Great Ship Company with a capital of £340,000. This new company then bought the *Great Eastern* for £160,000 on 15th February 1859. The shareholders in the old company were given the market value of their shares (which had plunged to 12 ½ per cent of their original value) and the Eastern Steam Navigation Company went into liquidation. By the time all was ready to start the fit-out of the ship, a year had elapsed.

Brunel had prepared the tenders for the fit-out work, but, diagnosed with Bright's disease (a disease of the kidneys), he was on his way to Egypt in the hope of improving his health when the bids came in. Two offers were received – one for £142,000 and one for £125,000. The lower tenderer was none other than John Scott Russell. He was awarded the contract for fit out with a premium of £1,000 a week for early delivery and a penalty of £10,000 a week for late delivery. When Brunel returned to England in May, whatever he felt about working again with Russell, he threw himself into supervising the fit-out.

The firm sub-contracted for the interior fit-out of the public rooms was Frederick Crace & Son of 14 Wigmore Street London, a long established firm of interior decorators. Frederick's father had begun in coach decoration before moving to interior furnishings. Frederick's son, John now headed up the firm. He had visited Paris in 1837 and on his return decorated the firm's Wigmore Street showroom in the French Renaissance style. His client list was impressive, including the Duke of Devonshire to whom the firm supplied carpets, upholstery, painted wall and ceilings for Chatsworth House. Frederick worked with Pugin on Alton Towers (home of the earls of Shrewsbury) and even made Gothic style furnishings for Pugin's own house in Ramsgate. The firm subsequently were awarded the contract for painting and gilding the New Palace of Westminster in 1846. The interior was described in a guidebook to the ship being:

> 'as if five hotels, each measuring about 80 ft x 60 ft and 25 ft high, were let down into an equal number of vast iron boxes. The separate compartments into which the 'hotels' for the accommodation of passengers are divided are as distinct from each other as so many different houses; each will have its splendid saloons, its bedrooms, or cabins, its kitchen, and its bar; and the passengers will no more be able to walk from the one to the other than the inhabitants of one house in Westbourne Terrace could communicate through the party walls with their next door neighbours. The only process by which visiting can be carried on will be by means of the upper deck or main thoroughfare of the ship.

Photographed by Robert Howlett, at one of the launch attempts, Brunel (right) stands under a tarpaulin with L-R, probably John Trotman the anchor maker, Lord Carlisle, Lord Alfred Paget and Mr Yates.

Most of the press was sympathetic with Brunel's struggle to launch the ship, and even this satirical cartoon, entitled 'A suggestion' stated 'This print is with every feeling of Sympathy, &c.' It almost predicts the ship's final years.

The Grand Saloon was 63 ft long, 47 ft wide and 14 ft high.

A very peculiar feature in this unique saloon is the mode by which it is lighted and ventilated at the sides – by large openings railed off with gilt balustrades, and reaching to the upper deck, where they are met by skylights, which can be left up or down at pleasure. Besides the great additional light which these openings give, they are invaluable as securing at any moment currents of fresh air.'

It also meant that light and air reached the deck below.

On either side of the saloon was a balcony supported by light iron columns with intricately designed balustrades – all the work of the Coalbrookedale Iron Company - treated to give the appearance of oxidised silver. The columns were made to look as if they were supporting the beams of the ship, which were decorated alternately in blue and red with the underside in gold. The panels between the beams were lightly decorated in gold.

The walls were hung with a fabric, richly patterned in gold and white, and divided into panels by green stiles and pilasters in imitation oxidised silver to match the columns.

The two funnels that ran through the room were hidden behind by octagonal casings. The longer sides were covered with mirrors, which made the room seem even larger. The smaller sides were fitted with arabesque panels ornamented with images of children and emblems of the sea. Mirrors also disguised the large airshafts at the sides of the saloon, with two faces covered with more arabesque paintings with children, this time personifying the arts and sciences connected with the building and navigation of the ship.

All doorways had *portières* of rich crimson silk; the carpet was maroon and of a simple pattern to highlight the other decoration. The sofas were covered with Utrecht velvet – a strong thick, pressed and crimped velvet. The buffet tables were of richly-carved walnut with green marble tops.

The Grand Saloon was reserved for the 'extra' first class passengers and ladies, but next to it was another saloon, even longer, that the 'ordinary' first class passengers could use. On either side of these two principal saloons was the accommodation for the passengers. They were more than cabins – they were suites, with sleeping, sitting, and dressing rooms, '*offering*', as the guide book describes them, *'to females as complete seclusion as if they were in their own homes. The smallest of these berths is larger than the best cabins in any other vessel; and they have the peculiar advantage of being at least double the height, and possessing most ample and ready means of ventilation.'*

Family cabins were 18 ft by 7 ft 6 in. and 7 ft 6 in. high.

The spacious and luxurious accommodation on board

I.K. Brunel on the deck of the Great Eastern, 5th September 1859. This is the last photograph taken of him. Seconds later, he collapsed and within ten days he was dead.

'The berths are so constructed that by a very simple process they can be made to collapse and fold together against the sides of the cabin, leaving a space of six inches between the two, so as to admit of stowing away the bedclothes; this done, curtains are drawn across, and so kept until night, the consequence being not only that the bed arrangements are entirely concealed all day, and the cabin turned into a snug little drawing-room, but that space is gained equal to about one-third of the whole area. The tables are so arranged as to be capable of extension or diminution in size. The cabins are floored with oilcloth, with Turkey rugs above. Under one of the settees is a bath, which can be easily supplied with hot fresh or salt water, by the aid of what are called the 'donkey-engines' or some of the multitudinous shaftings which are to work everything all over the ship.'

On the lower deck, the saloons were simpler in decoration than those above, as were the cabins. All efforts had been made to keep the accommodation and public rooms close to the centre of the ship, where the roll of the vessel would be felt less. The crew accommodation was in the bow, the captain's and officers' in the stern.

At the end of August 1859 the *Great Eastern,* finished and fitted out in a style of shipboard luxury undreamt of, was crewed, coaled and prepared for trials.

September 1859: the maiden voyage begins

The *Great Eastern* was conceived as a ship to travel to Australia and the Far East. However, the cost of fitting out the ship left the Great Ship Company without the money to finance such a long voyage. Worse, the extent of Australia's vast coal reserves were beginning to be discovered and exploited – there was no longer a need for a ship that could sail there and back to England without refuelling. Instead, the Great Ship Company looked west, to the transatlantic trade.

Brunel continued to visit the ship as frequently as he could, even taking a house in Sydenham (where Russell also had a house) to be closer. 30th August 1859 was the date set for the *Great Eastern*'s maiden voyage, although this was put back to 6th September. Brunel was now very seriously ill, but came on board on the 5th. It was his last visit to his Great Babe: towards midday, he collapsed and

Guided by tugs the *Great Eastern* sails down the Thames on 7th September 1859, accompanied by a flotilla of small boats, to begin her maiden voyage

was taken home. Although he had planned to be on board for the maiden voyage, he was simply not well enough.

The *Great Eastern*'s destination was to be Weymouth (cabins were available at £6 and £10) and from there she would travel on to Holyhead on Anglesey from where she would depart for America on 30th September. Holyhead was chosen as the port of departure to some extent because several of the directors were large shareholders in London & North West Railway that served the port. The *Great Eastern* would then sail to Portland, Maine, where the Grand Trunk Railway of Canada had agreed to build a new jetty to receive her.

This first voyage was also to be her sea trial – the measure of performance and seaworthiness every vessel undergoes, but not usually as part of a maiden voyage. Some 150 to 200 passengers boarded her on 5th, but it was not until 7.30 a.m. on 7th September, the steam tugs *Victoria* and *Napoleon* pulled the *Great Eastern* into the middle of the Thames (with the tugs *Punch* and *Victor* at her stern) and the voyage began. The river was so crowded that her commander, Captain Harrison, decided to moor at Purfleet for the night. It was the next day that the ship, accompanied by hundreds of small boats, finally left the Thames for the open sea.

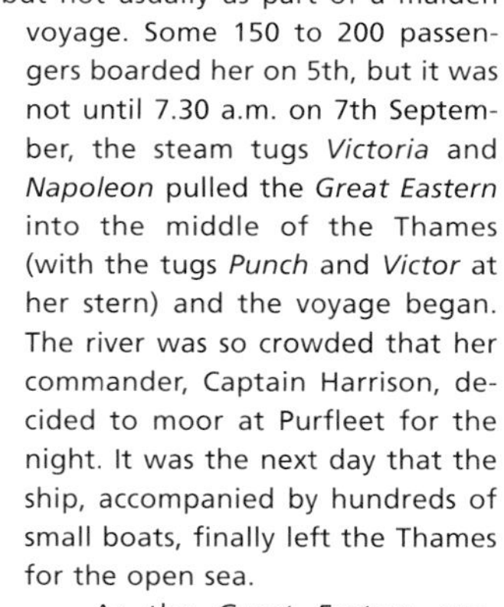

As the *Great Eastern* progressed, it became clear that there was a problem with the engines that fed water to the boilers. The officer of the watch on duty in the paddle engine room decided to solve this by shutting off the water that was supplied, pre-heated,

A coloured lithograph dramatically reconstructing the explosion on board on 9th September 1859. The artist has brought the ship close to the shore: she was in fact several miles off land.

The remains of the forward funnel after the explosion

from the water tanks that jacketed the two forward-most funnels. Stop cocks were closed at both ends. Consequently the water became hotter and hotter. The inevitable explosion occurred at 6:00 p.m., just after passengers had dined, as the ship was passing seven miles off shore from Hastings. The forward funnel was completely blown off and as it rose it destroyed the Grand Saloon through which it passed. Eleven men were caught in the steam that blew back into the boiler room. One was so badly scalded that he jumped overboard, only to be entangled in the paddle wheels and killed. Two more died on board, John Boyd and Michael Mahon, and three were to die the following day in Weymouth Hospital.

The Times reported:

> 'The fore part of Mr Crace's beautiful saloon was a pile of glittering rubbish, a mere confused mass of boards, carpet shreds, hangings, mirrors, gilt frames and splinters of ornaments; the rich gilt castings were broken and thrown down, the brass work ripped, the handsome iron columns around the funnel overturned and strewn about.'

There was only one person in the Grand Saloon at the time – the young daughter of William Harrison, the ship's captain. Miraculously, she was unharmed. One of the engineers, realising what happened, checked the other stop cock, and opened it and so prevented a second explosion. But, disastrous though it was, one author reported 'No other ship afloat could have withstood the enormous bursting pressure of the steam, nor have survived the shock; and yet it is a literal and actual fact that *no harm whatever* has been done to any part of the fabric. ... [In] the next compartment but one the shock experienced was no more, as one of the gentlemen present expressed it, than if one of the crew passing overhead with a twelve-pound shot in his hands had let it fall to the deck.'

Brunel received the news of the tragedy on 10th September. It is unlikely that it hastened his death which came five days later, but it would certainly have affected him deeply.

Knowing that the ship was not in danger, Captain Harrison proceeded to Weymouth where his passengers disembarked and were given a refund. John Scott Russell once again proved optimistic with costing, estimating £5,000 for the repairs needed when it would actually cost £18,000. To offset the costs a little the Great Ship Company opened her to the public as an attraction.

One Sunday while the ship lay at anchor off Weymouth, the crew, perhaps still disconcerted by the explosion, refused to wash the decks, considering it neither necessary nor within the articles of their employment. Captain Harrison took this very seriously and had a number of them brought before the County magistrates on a charge of mutinous conduct. Most were imprisoned for a fortnight with hard labour, but the alleged 'ringleader' received a month in Dorchester gaol.

October 1859: the Great Charter Storm

Fully repaired and with a new crew, the ship made a short sea trial before leaving for Holyhead on the afternoon of 15th October. Once off the coast of Anglesey, she was again opened to visitors while preparations were made for the voyage to America.

The strength of the ship was tested once more on the night of 25th-26th October, when a huge storm hit Holyhead. It became known as the 'Royal Charter storm' after the most prominent of the 133 ships sunk that night. The steamship *Royal Charter*, returning from Australia with a large quantity of gold, was wrecked on the rocks with the loss of over 450 lives. Very few of those on board were rescued and in total an estimated 800 lives were lost. On the *Great Eastern*, Captain Harrison kept his engines running, holding the bow into the storm and keeping the ship out of trouble. Nevertheless the Great Ship Company was so disturbed by the Royal Charter storm that they decided Southampton, not Holyhead, would be the port of departures for their ship's transatlantic voyages. And she would sail to New York, not to Portland Maine as the Great Ship Company had promised. The Grand Trunk Railway of Canada who had built the new pier at Portland were understandably furious.

So on 2nd November 1859 the *Great Eastern* retraced her route round the Welsh and English coasts back to Southampton. And once more she was anchored and inactive. A new board was appointed and with an increase in capital some of the defects in the ship were addressed, mostly to do with the paddle engines. The work was undertaken by Langley, Penn & Field who had designed the ship's steering apparatus.

January 1860: Captain Harrison drowns

Then another tragedy struck. On 21st January 1860, Captain Harrison, who had been appointed captain in 1856 while the ship was still being built, was in one of the *Great Eastern*'s boats – the captain's gig – along with ship's doctor Dr Watson; Charles Ogden the coxswain, Captain Ley the superintendent purser and his young son, and five of the ship's crew. They had set out from Hythe, where Harrison's family were living, and were nearing the entrance to Southampton's docks when a sudden gust of wind caught the sail and overturned the boat. Harrison, the coxswain and the purser's son were all drowned. *The Times* described is as '[a] nother most tragic incident … added to the long list of catastrophes which seem to have dogged the course of this ill-fated vessel from the very first day of her existence.'

Captain Harrison standing beside the Great *Eastern's* compass binnacle. His career as a captain began in ships sailing to Barbados but for more than 12 years he captained Cunard packet boats sailing between Liverpool and New York.

June 1860: first voyage to North America begins

The Company appointed John Vine Hall, an experienced officer in the East India trade but who had never made a transatlantic crossing, to replace Harrison as captain. The passengers were few for the first transatlantic voyage: around 20, but including Daniel Gooch, who had been Brunel's 'superintendent of locomotives' and was now a director of the Great Ship Company. He may have been disappointed by a delayed departure to 17th June because of a drunken crew and by Captain Vine taking a southerly route and consequently almost 11 days to complete the voyage, but he was heartened by the hundreds of yachts and steamers that turned out to accompany the ship into New York, by the thousands of spectators who

The *Great Eastern* in the United States

lined the banks of the Hudson and by the gun salutes from the ships of the United States Navy.

On 3rd July the ship was opened up to the public and by the end of the month 140,000 visitors had come on board. Gooch was heavily involved in promoting the ship but later conceded 'I cannot say, now it is all over, that we were very clever at our work.' A two-day excursion took 1,500 passengers to Cape May but failed to impress the journalists on board. Gooch enjoyed a second, press-free trip more, but there were only a hundred passengers on board. Nevertheless, the ship attracted huge attention wherever she went – even President Buchanan and his cabinet visited, taking lunch on board. The Company then heard that the ship would be welcomed in Halifax, Nova Scotia. Off she sailed, making the quickest passage on record ... only to be handed a bill for £350 from the Halifax harbour authorities for light dues. The *Great Eastern* left for home the next morning, 19th August, but with only 72 passengers. Her destination was Milford Haven – the only place with a gridiron large enough for her – where she spent the winter. The captain and all but twelve of the crew were discharged.

June 1861: Great Eastern becomes a troopship

On 1st May 1861, the *Great Eastern* sailed from Milford Haven across the Atlantic with 100 passengers. She did not stay in New York long, departing on 25th May. There was little interest in the ship now: the American public were preoccupied with the Civil War that had broken out on 10th April that year. In Britain there was a fear that this conflict might spread to Canada, partly because the border with Northern states of the Union was ill-defined in places and partly because there was an undisguised sympathy for the Confederate states among a large number of Britons – including prominent Liberal politicians – who believed Northern aggression and not the issue of slavery was the real cause of the war. With only a single regular battalion stationed in Canada, it

In 1861, the *Great Eastern* became a troop ship, ferrying men across the Atlantic to defend Canada against possible invasion by the United States

was decided to reinforce it with the 4th Battalion 60th Rifles and a battery of the Royal Artillery. The *Great Eastern* was chartered to convey two thousand, one hundred and forty-four officers and men, 473 women and children and 200 horses. With another forty paying passengers on board, the ship left Liverpool on 25th June 1861.

About a hundred of the crew had been pressed into service and on the first morning at sea, they refused to work. The new captain of the ship, James Kennedy, identified the ringleaders and had the troops on board force them into the rigging at bayonet point, where they stayed all day. Neither crew nor weather deterred Captain Kennedy and he reached Quebec in just eight days and six hours.

The *Great Eastern* returned to Liverpool with 357 paying passengers and after a period on the gridiron in Milford Haven she was prepared for a second voyage to America. Finance was again a problem: £35,000 had to be raised by debentures to pay Russell's bill and to fund the next voyage. The Grand Trunk Railroad of Canada was also threatening to sue for breach of contract over the failure to sail to Portland, Maine. To save money, the Great Ship Company dismissed six of the ten senior officers and a third of the crew. Captain Carnegie, Kennedy's replacement resigned. A new captain was found, William B. Thompson, but not many passengers: only 100 booked from Milford Haven to New York , and only 194 booked for the return voyage to England.

September 1861: an aborted voyage to New York

For the next voyage, James Walker was appointed captain. Four hundred passengers were on board as the ship departed from Liverpool on 10th September. On the second day out the ship began to roll and it was discovered that the port paddle wheel had been damaged – the floats were broken and the wheel was scraping against the hull. Unfortunately the screw engine alone was not powerful enough to hold the ship into the wind, and she turned broadside to the waves. The port paddle wheel then disappeared under water and broke off. Next, over

The *Great Eastern* had a reputation for being uncomfortable in a storm, but there is no record of a bull crashing through a skylight as the artist would have us believe

the following three days, all the ship's boats broke away. And then, the top of the rudder post had sheared off and the rudder was swinging free, useless and rubbing against the propeller which was gradually destroying it. But worst of all the cargo had not been stowed properly and was now shifting. The *Great Eastern* was in real danger of capsize.

All the measures Captain Walker took proved ineffective and finally he was forced to agree to a plan developed by one of the passengers, Hamilton E. Towle, an American civil engineer, to regain control of the rudder using a system of chains. A degree of control was achieved, but not enough for the harbour master at Queenstown to allow the ship to enter. She was eventually towed in by H.M.S. *Advice* but even with this assistance a quartermaster was killed by the sudden movement of the wheel. The final episode in this catalogue of disasters was the ship's collision in the harbour with the barque S*amuel Maxley*, damaging the small vessel's stern.

The voyage was abandoned, with the passengers offered free transport on other ships and while repairs were being made the ship opened again to the paying public. Once back home in America, Towle put in a claim for salvage (as he had brought a drifting ship under control) and was awarded $15,000.

May 1862–August 1863: transatlantic voyages

New, smaller paddle wheels were now installed, 50 ft in diameter, and under the command of Captain John Paton, the *Great Eastern* left Milford Haven on 7th May 1862 for New York with 138 passengers. Arriving ten days later, the previous year's preoccupation with the war and any anti-British sentiments had evaporated and around 3,000 visitors came on board to see the ship every day. The return journey took 389 passengers on a record

The *Great Eastern* at Heart's Content, Newfoundland, in July 1866 just after she had laid the first submarine transatlantic telegraph cable

breaking 9 days 12 hours. When a second voyage that year also brought a successful number of passengers and cargo, it seemed that a corner had been turned. But on the third voyage in the early hours of 28th August 1862, arriving off Montauk Point, just after Paton took a pilot on board off Montauk Point, there was the sound of a rumble and the ship started to heel slightly to port. She scraped the North East Ripps, later renamed the Great Eastern Rock.

Although no leak was detected, once the passengers and cargo were unloaded Captain Paton ordered an inspection. This revealed a gash 80ft long and 4ft wide. A lesser puncture in the hull sank the *Titanic*, but not the *Great Eastern*. It did however take three months to repair – partly because of the need to build a caisson (a structure that could be pumped out to create a temporary dry dock) around the ship to get at the damaged plates and partly because of the shortage of iron caused by the on-going Civil War.

It was not until January 1863 that the ship departed. She left New York with around 1,200 passengers and arrived in Liverpool with one more: Captain Paton's wife Eliza had given birth to a son.

Although three return voyages were made in 1863 with good passenger numbers, the Great Ship Company was became a victim of a price war that was being waged at the time between the two great shipping lines, Cunard and Inman. The Company was losing money – nearly £20,000 on these voyages alone. With debts totalling over £142,000, even with large numbers of passengers the Great Ship Company could not run the *Great Eastern* profitably.

Great Eastern's first visit to New York: a stagecoach from the nearby Western Hotel brings sightseers. The photographer may have been George Stacy, best known for his Civil War photographs of Fort Monroe, Virginia.

June 1865-September 1866: the Atlantic cable layer

The Great Ship Company was desperate to rid itself of the ship. First it attempted to offer the ship in a lottery in Frankfurt (as lotteries were illegal in Britain) but when this fell through the *Great Eastern* was put up for sale on 14th January 1864 in the Cotton Room in the Liverpool Exchange. Unfortunately when the auctioneer opened the bidding at the reserve of £50,000 there were no takers. It was then announced that the ship would be auctioned again in three weeks, but this time with no reserve.

But one of the Great Ship Company's directors, Brunel's old friend Daniel Gooch, did see a future for her. He had been in talks with Cyrus Field, the American entrepreneur who had laid the first transatlantic cable in 1858. This cable had successfully transmitted over 700 messages between 13th August and 20th October when it failed: Field was now planning to lay a second, more durable cable, and he needed a large ship. So Gooch formed a small group to buy the *Great Eastern*. Although they were prepared to go as high as £80,000, they bought the ship for a mere £25,000, a quarter of its value in materials if she had been scrapped. Gooch and his partners formed a new firm – the Great Eastern Steamship Company – and chartered out to the equally newly-formed Telegraph Construction & Maintenance Company in return for shares. The charterers were also responsible for converting the ship into a cable layer.

The *Great Eastern* was now fitted with three enormous circular storage tanks capable of holding in total 2,490 nautical miles of cable and, under Captain James Anderson, she left Sheerness on 24th June 1865 for Valentia, one of Ireland's most westerly points. She successfully laid over 1,000 nautical miles of cable and was only 607 nautical miles from her destination, Heart's Content on the Canadian island of Labrador, when the cable broke. Five days were spent trying to recover the end of cable from the seabed 2,000 fathoms below. Although located, it proved impossible to recover it.

The *Great Eastern* headed back east. She had been out of contact for so long that when she arrived at Crookhaven, on the southern tip of Ireland, on 17th August she received the message: 'We did not know what to make of you. Many think you went down.'

The following year the *Great Eastern* was chartered by Anglo-American Telegraph Company – a new company but one set up by Cyrus Field to circumvent

Inside one of the giant tanks where the telegraph cable was stored and payed out through a hatch

Lowering a buoy to mark the position where the cable broke. At the bow, a grapnel is ready to be lowered to attempt to recover the cable.

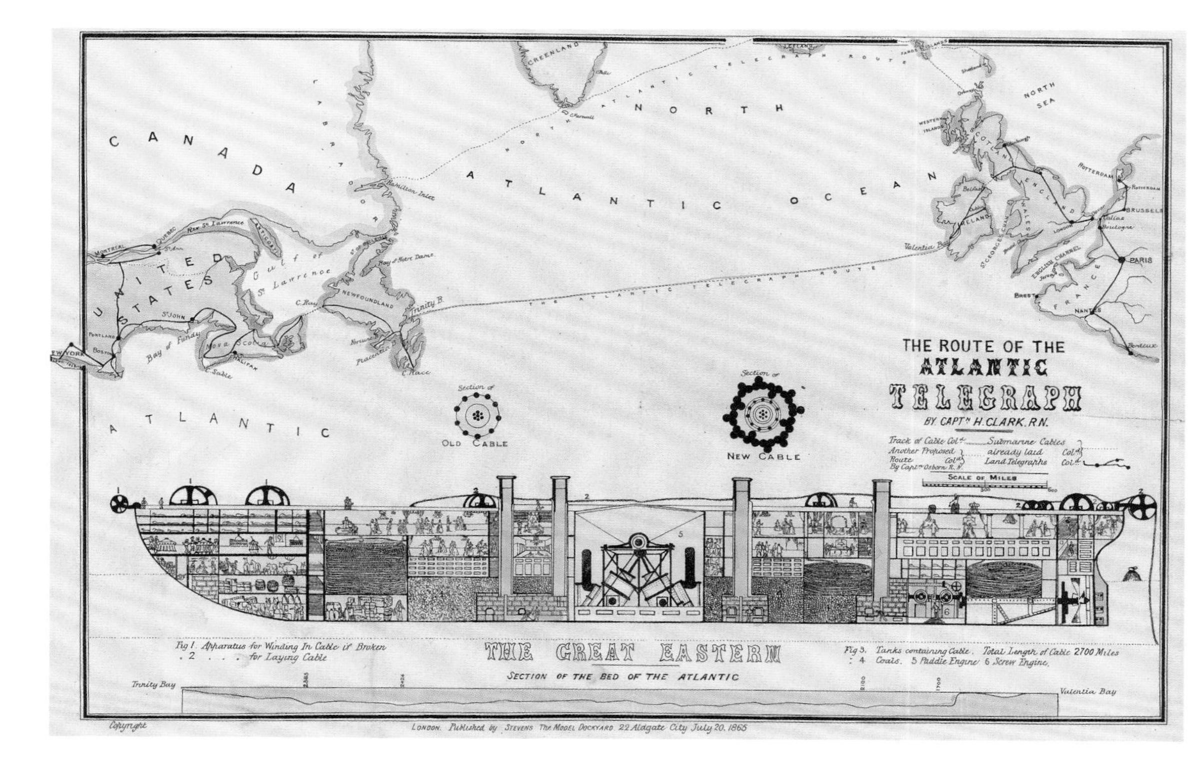

A hand-coloured etching that combines a chart of the route of the transatlantic cable with a cutaway of the ship. It shows how the *Great Eastern* was fitted out as a cable layer, but also some of her former glory, including couples dancing and horses being transported. Printed in 1865.

British government restrictions on raising capital. Cable laying began off Valencia on 13th July 1866. Fourteen days later, on 27th July, after only a couple of minor incidents, the laying was complete and the *Great Eastern* steamed into Heart's Content. The cable was a success.

However, there was still a valuable cable lying at the bottom of the sea unused – the broken 1865 cable. *Great Eastern* now helped in its recovery and repair. And by early September two transatlantic cables were operational, thanks to the *Great Eastern*.

March 1867: the French Expo charter

1867 was the year of the International Exposition in Paris, with over 50,000 exhibitors. The *Great Eastern* was leased, for £1,000 a month, by La Société des Affréteurs du Great Eastern, to bring wealthy Americans across the Atlantic to France. However, the cable gear and tanks had to be stripped out, the engines overhauled, power steering fitted and three additional dining saloons were built on the main deck: works which cost around £80,000.

Around a thousand passengers booked on the outward voyage from Liverpool to New York, including the novelist Jules Verne. In 1871 he published *Une*

Ville Flottante (*A Floating City*): an improbable romantic story to which a factual description of the *Great Eastern* was interwoven.

As the raising of the anchor began, Verne was standing *with several other passengers, watching the details of the departure. Near me stood a traveller, who frequently shrugged his shoulders impatiently and did not spare disparaging jokes on the tardiness of the work* [being performed by a 66-h.p. donkey engines and 50 crewmen on the capstan]. *"I thought by now, sir," said he to me, "that engines were made to help men, not men to help engines."*

> I was going to reply to this wise observation, when there was a loud cry, and immediately my companion and I were hurled towards the bows; every man at the capstan bars was knocked down; some got up again, others laid scattered on the deck. A catch had broken, and the capstan being forced round by the frightful pressure of the chains, the men, caught on the rebound, were struck violently on the head and chest. Freed from their broken rope-bands, the capstan-bars flew in all directions like grape-shot, killing four sailors and wounding twelve others; among the latter was the boatswain, a Scotchman from Dundee.
>
> The spectators hurried towards the unfortunate men, the wounded were taken to the hospital at the stern; as for the four already dead, preparations were immediately made to send them on shore; so lightly do Anglo-Saxons regard death, that this event made very little impression on board. These unhappy men, killed and wounded, were only tools, which could be replaced at very little expense.

Illustration from Jules Verne's *Une Ville Flottante (A Floating City)* showing life aboard the *Great Eastern*

Verne gives a vivid portrait of life on board:

> ... I had chosen my cabin at the bows; it was a small room well lit by two skylights. A second row of cabins separated it from the first saloon, so that neither the noise of conversation , nor the rattling of pianos, which were not wanting on board, could disturb me. It was an isolated cabin; the furniture consisted of a sofa, a bedstead, and a toilet-table.
>
> The first care of each passenger, when he had once set foot on the steamer, was to go and secure his place in the dining-room; his card or his

name written on a scrap of paper, was enough to secure his possession... Four times a day, to the great satisfaction of the passengers, [a] shrill horn sounded: at half-past eight for breakfast, half-past twelve for lunch, four o'clock for dinner, and at seven for tea. In a few minutes the long streets were deserted, and soon the tables in the immense saloons were filled with guests... The dining-rooms were provided with four long rows of tables; the glasses and bottles placed in swing-racks kept perfectly steady; the roll of the steamer was almost imperceptible, so that the guests–men women and children–- could eat their lunch without any fear. Numerous waiters were busy carrying round the tastily-arranged dishes, and supplying the demands for wine and beer; the Californians certainly distinguished themselves by their proclivities for champagne.... two or three pale, delicate-looking young ladies were eagerly devouring slices of red beef; and others discussed with evident satisfaction the merits of rhubarb tarts, &c. Every one worked away in the highest spirits; one could have fancied oneself at a restaurant in the middle of Paris.

Lunch over, the decks filled again; people bowed and spoke to each other in passing as formally as if they were walking in Hyde Park; children played and ran about, throwing their balls and bowling hoops as they might have done on the gravel walks of the Tuileries; the greater part of the men walked up and down smoking; the ladies, seated on folding chairs, worked, read, or talked together, whilst the governesses and nurses looked after the children. A few corpulent Americans swung themselves backwards and forwards in their rocking chairs, the ship's officers were continually passing to and fro, some going to their watch on the bridge, others answering the absurd questions put to them by some of the passengers; whilst the tones of an organ and two or three pianos making a distracting discord, reached us through the lulls in the wind.

The ship later gets into rough seas, but Verne still cannot escape the noise of keyboards *:*

From Sheerness to Valentia by Robert Dudley. A view of the deck as the Great *Eastern* sailed to the west coast of Ireland in 1865 to begin cable laying. Dudley was the expedition artist.

> When the weather was favourable, the boulevards were thronged with promenaders, who managed to maintain the perpendicular, in spite of the ship's motion, but with the peculiar gyrations of tipsy men. When the passengers did not go on deck, they remained either in their private sitting-rooms or in the grand saloon, and then began the noisy discords of pianos, all played at the same time, which, however, seemed not to affect Saxon ears in the least.'

Verne was not entirely in awe of the ship's power and disappointed with the ship's speed. One of the book's characters remarks, on seeing a young couple very much in love and travelling to America to marry, *'Ah! sir, if our boilers were heated like those two youthful hearts, see how our speed would increase!'*

Disastrously, when the ship arrived in New York, there were not the 4,000 passengers expected to travel to France – only 191. The company was now in a dire financial position, so much so that after the ship crossed the Atlantic and was standing off Brest, Captain Anderson would allow no visitors on board in case they turned out to be creditors who might seize the ship. Returning to Liverpool, the crew were discharged in Liverpool and told to sue the French company (which was bankrupt) for their wages. However, after affidavits were presented to the Court of Admiralty, the *Great Eastern* was seized in lieu of a claim for £4,500 in unpaid wages. The Great Eastern Steamship Company now offered £1,500, which the crew accepted. Captain Anderson's troubles were not entirely over – he had to appear at the Liverpool Police Court to answer a claim of £21,000 from local traders who had worked on or provisioned the ship. He cleverly evaded replying by stating that no claims could be paid until all the liabilities were known and then the Great Eastern Steamship Company would sue La Société des Affréteurs du Great Eastern.

1869 –1874: return to cable laying

But the *Great Eastern* was not finished; indeed her next employer was another French company, La Sociéte du Câble Transatlantique Française. After the success of the British cables, the French also wanted a cable to America. The *Great Eastern* was converted back into a cable layer, with an even bigger main tank to cope with the longer cable that was needed. Departing from Brest on 20th June 1869 she arrived off St Pierre on 12th of July. Another cable had been successfully laid with very little drama.

The *Great Eastern* seemed finally to have found a role. Her next task was to lay almost 2,000 nautical miles of cable between Bombay and Aden, but not before opening up to Indian visitors at two rupees a head. For this work in the tropics, the captain, Robert Halpin, had the ship painted white to reduce the temperature below decks, which it is said it did by 8 degrees farenheit.

Her final task was to lay 325 miles of cable in the Red Sea, before returning to Liverpool. And there she was to remain for the next three years.

The *Great Eastern* undertook just two more cable laying voyage: in 1873 she laid another cable between Valentia and Heart's Content, then the following year lay a cable in the other direction, from Heart's Content to Valentia. This was to turn out to be the last of her true seafaring activities.

The *Great Eastern* laid up in Milford Haven in the 1870s

1874-1886: at Milford Haven

The *Great Eastern* returned to Milford Haven to be beached. In 1876 she was used as a platform for pile driving for a new dry dock, which, for convenience, was built around her. Unfortunately once the dock was completed it was discovered that the dock gates were too narrow for the ship to leave without removing her paddle boxes. The expense of this and their reinstatement swallowed up any profit made for being a pile-driving platform. She became an attraction for sightseers, although not open to the public.

In the twelve years at Milford Haven, many schemes were concocted for the ship's future but none came to fruition. Gooch finally left the Great Eastern Steamship Company in 1880. In September the following year the *Great Eastern* was put up for sale. The reserve price was £75,000; the best offer was £30,000, (still more than the Great Eastern Steamship Company had paid for her) and she remained unsold. (Although no longer connected with the ship, her builder John Scott Russell died 'in reduced circumstances' at Ventnor in 1882.)

In 1883 there was a possibility of the ship going to America as part of the New Orleans Exhibition. But the Great Eastern Steamship Company acting chairman, Barber, and a co-director, Marsden, were arrested and charged with fraud and bribery over the deal.

1886 – 1887: showboat

By order of the High Court of Justice, the *Great Eastern* was auctioned on 28th October 1885. She was sold to Edward de Mattos on behalf of the London Traders Company, of which he was the managing director. De Mattos had offered £50,000 in 1883 but now secured her for £26,200 and she seemed destined to become a coal hulk at Gibraltar. However, Louis S. Cohen of Lewis's department store in Liverpool, who had made an unsuccessful bid of £20,000 at the auction, now offered to charter her for the summer on condition that she was available for the 1886 Liverpool Exhibition of Navigation, Travelling, Commerce and Manufactures, which was to be opened by Queen Victoria on 11th May 1886. It was hoped that she would visit the ship (she had after all visited it at Deptford when it was being fitted out), although in the event she did not.

Cohen arranged a party of 200 to travel on the ship from Milford Haven to Liverpool but the paddle engines were by then beyond repair, and the screw engine little better, continually stopping. But eventually she reached Liverpool by which time her port side (facing Birkenhead) had the letters 'LADIES SHOULD VISIT LEWIS'S BON MARCHE CHURCH STREET' and the starboard side (facing Liverpool) towards the stern 'LEWIS'S ARE THE FRIENDS OF THE PEOPLE', with the name LEWIS in letters 30 ft high and towards the bow:

> RANELAGH STREET LEWIS'S BON MARCHE
> LIVERPOOL BASENETT STREET
> MANCHESTER, SHEFFIELD, BIRMINGHAM

She arrived on 1st May, and anchored close to Rock Ferry. The cable tanks became music halls and dance halls, the Grand Saloon a bar and the Ladies Saloon a dining room. Stalls and sideshows filled the ship, while trapeze artists performed on the main deck between the Tuesday and Wednesday masts. Acts included Miss

Annie Foxcroft, vocalist; Gus and Julia Connolley and the Templetons, sketch artists; Tom Coyne, eccentric comedian; Cyrus and Maude, musical grotesques; Petit Syd, trapeze performer; Leonard White and Bertie Roseland, burlesque artists; Mons. Derkaro, the Japanese Wonder; Louise and Elba, flying gymnasts; Richard Lee, contortionist; W.H. Vane, the banjo king; Miss Nelly Fletcher, skipping rope dancer; Smith and Orton, 'Negro comedians'; Harry Pleon, character comedian; Captain Manard, with his sensational rifle shooting performance; Beautiful Ariel, introduced by Professor Hubner; and Major Devono, in his conjuring show.

The *Great Eastern* was open twelve hours a day (and on one day 14 hours), seven days a week, illuminated in the evenings by electric light. In the first month 50,000 visitors came on board and 20,000 during the Whitsun Bank Holiday. By the end of August, more than 370,000 people had paid a shilling to visit the ship.

In 1886 the hull of the ship became an advertising hoarding with a fairground inboard

A cramped dining saloon (upper) and a less luxurious saloon (lower) on the *Great Eastern*. These photographs were taken in late 1886 or early 1887 when the ship was berthed at North Wall, Dublin. Note how the chandeliers are crudely restrained by ropes after, or in anticipation of, a rough sea crossing.

Sunday opening of course attracted the attention of the Working Men's Lord's Day Rest Association, who, correctly deducing this was illegal, served a writ on the London Traders Company. De Mattos wrote to the *Liverpool Mercury* that the ship was chartered so they had no power to intervene. He continued, 'the sacred music hitherto held on board on Sundays has been stopped. Although the number visiting the ship is very large, her spacious decks afford sufficient room on board for an even greater number, so that any one anxious to visit the vessel can readily do so without the necessity existing of trenching on the quietude and rest of the Sunday.'

Seeing Cohen's success, others thought they could do the same and sought to launch a public company, the Great Eastern Steamship (Exhibition & Entertainment) Company Limited, but it failed to raise the £100,000 capital needed. Undaunted, after the contract expired with Cohen had expired, the London Traders Company took the ship to Dublin, where she arrived on 14th October. But lacking the amusements that had been on board during her time at Liverpool, and crucially lacking a licence to sell alcohol, it was a commercial failure. Between October and the end of March she attracted a mere 40,000 visitors. The *Great Eastern* was sold on 17th February to two Manchester businessmen, Messrs. Worsley and Brocklehurst, and by April 1887 she was back in Liverpool. However, for no other reason than protecting the interest of publicans in Liverpool, the new owners were refused a licence to sell alcohol here too.

The ship re-opened as an attraction briefly but on 20th October 1887 she was auctioned once again in Liverpool and bought for £21,000 by a Mr Craik, a manager working for Mr Worsley, presumably to prevent her from being sold too cheaply. It was however a very short term measure. Auctioned again on 15th December, she was sold for £16,500 but the purchaser refused to pay a 10 per cent deposit and was the offer was withdrawn.

The *Great Eastern* was now taken to the Clyde and moored between Helensburgh and Greenock and again reopened as a visitor attraction, but with even less success. Nevertheless, the press at least believed the ship had a future, reporting that she was going to be turned back into a passenger ship, or that she would visit Middlesborough and Southampton as a floating exhibition, or that P.T. Barnum had made an offer for her. None of these materialised.

Now the possession of a department store owner, signwriters emblazoned the ship with his advertisements: some of the letters were 30 feet high

The Last Voyage of the Great Eastern, by Charles W. Wylllie. The ship was brought from Glasgow to Birkenhead in 1888.

1888 – 1889: the final days of the Great Eastern

The *Great Eastern* was soon sold on, for £16,500, to Henry Bath & Sons, metal brokers who also ran shipbuilding and ship breaking businesses.

When the company executives saw the ship on the Clyde they initially considered putting new engines in her, possibly turning her into a cattle transporter or an oil tanker, but she was destined to be broken up. Shorn of her paddle wheels, the *Great Eastern* left the Clyde on 22nd August 1888 with a crew of 115 on board and accompanied by the Liverpool tugs *Stormcock* and *Pathfinder*. Her own engine struggled to make four or five knots. On the second day of the voyage, the vessels were caught in a gale. *Stormcock* cast loose her hawser and when the *Great Eastern*'s engines stopped briefly, she became unsteerable. For four hours she drifted, with seas breaking over her, even though she stood 40 feet out of the water. The storm abated on the following morning and the towing resumed. In all, the journey to Liverpool took three days.

Reaching the Mersey, every landing stage was crowded, and steamboats plied the river full of spectators wanting one more glimpse of the great ship before she was beached on the south side of New Ferry Pier, at Birkenhead on the Cheshire shore of the Mersey.

On 20th November a three-day auction was begun to sell off the ship's metals, engines, machinery, sails, ropes and rigging – every single element of the vessel. One successful bidder was the Anfield Football Stadium, then the home of

Everton F.C. In need of a flagpole, they secured the topmast of 'Thursday'. It remains there to this day, although the ground is now Liverpool F.C.'s.

Henry Bath & Sons made £25,000 from the plates, £7,000 from the copper and brass and £4,000 from the gunmetal. Souvenir hunters paid another £22,000. Their estimate was that it would cost £20,000 for 200 men to work around the clock for a year to break up the ship. Work on the demolition of the ship began in May 1889, but the double hull was much more resistant than anyone had anticipated. The solution was a new invention – the wrecking ball – and this was the first recorded use of the device. A large crane was set up over the ship and a stationary steam engine would hoist the wrecking ball to a certain height before it was released by a trigger. The impact sprung the rivets in the plates, allowing them to be separated. Even so, it took two years to break up the *Great Eastern*, not the one year Henry Bath & Sons planned. They were to join the list of those who made a loss from owning the ship.

Looking back at the Great Eastern

The *Great Eastern* never fulfilled the purpose for which she was built. She never sailed to Australia; she never took passengers to the East; she never took her full capacity of passengers anywhere. Her engines were not powerful enough for her size; she was not an effective competitor to the big shipping lines that dominated the Atlantic passenger trade. At a time when mass migration across the Atlantic and to the gold-fields of Australia was booming, she failed to capture any proportion of the market. To sail on the *Great Eastern* was a novelty, but not one many wanted to repeat. With the possible exception of the London Traders, every owner lost money on her.

She was a ship overtaken by events. At the time she was built, no-one predicted the vast coal deposits of Australia would negate the reason for the ship's vast size. She was too deep for the Suez Canal which opened in late 1869 (although when work began a decade earlier, few in Britain believed the canal would ever be completed). And no-one predicted the huge improvements that were to be made to the efficiency of marine engines.

But she was also hugely ahead of her time. It would not be until 1899, when the White Star Line's *Oceanic* was launched, that was there a ship longer than the *Great Eastern* and not until 1907, when Cunard launched the *Lusitania* was there

The 1888 auction. Note the auctioneer in Sketch 3 handing out free cigars to bidders.

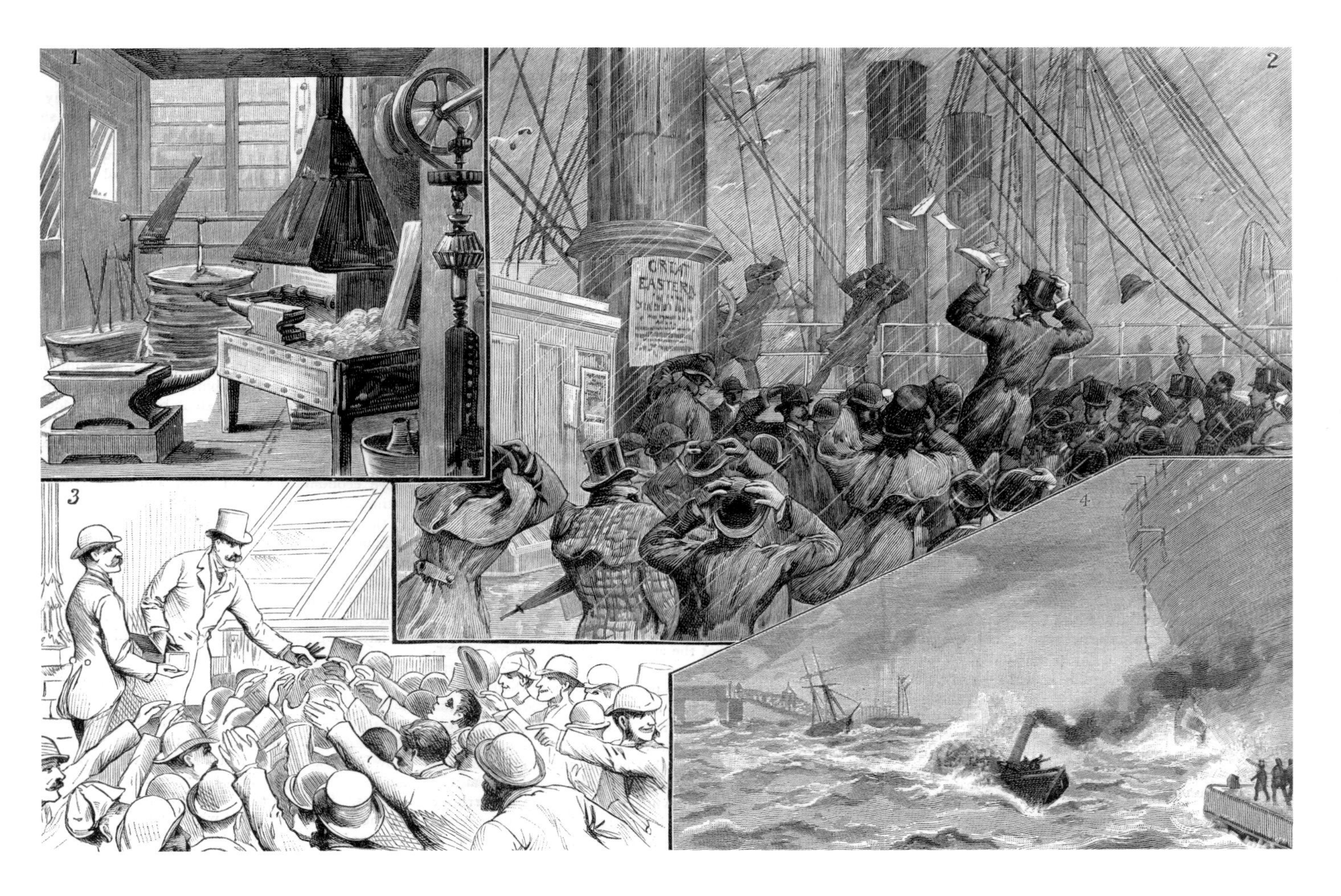

The breaking up of the *Great Eastern* by Henry Bath's men. It would take 3.5 million man-hours to accomplish.

a ship that exceeded her in tonnage. There was probably no safer ship than the *Great Eastern* until the sinking of the *Titanic* in 1912 shook shipbuilders out of their complacency.

The *Great Eastern* was Brunel's 'Great Babe', a project to which he probably devoted more time and energy than to any other. And for all the troubles she had brought him, John Scott Russell remained immensely proud of the *Great Eastern*. He had engaged photographers (P.H. Delamotte and later Robert Howlett) to record the construction and included illustrations of her in his massive three-volume *The Modern System of Naval Architecture*, published in 1864. He also had a number of the drawings used in the book hand-coloured and bound into presentation albums.

She may have been a commercial failure but she was an engineering triumph – pushing the technology of the day to the limit. She was the embodiment of the times – bigger, bolder and brighter than anything that had been put to sea before. From her construction to her final voyage to Birkenhead, she never failed to attract huge crowds to view this wonder of the age, but she was more than just a manifestation of the Victorian enthusiasm for novelty. She epitomised a new way of thinking, that problems and challenges should be solved without preconceptions or reverting to traditional practices. Iron ships did not have to be built like like wooden ships, but could be constructed in new ways to exploit the strength of the material. Even though the problem of coal shortages on the route to Australia was soon to vanish, the solution was uncompromisingly brilliant– a ship inconceivably large. The *Great Eastern* is the literally the biggest example of rational problem solving. And this approach changed everything in the modern world.

OVERLEAF
One of the last photographs of the *Great Eastern*, beached at Rock Ferry on the Mersey, waiting to be broken up

GREAT EASTERN

The *Great Eastern* in figures

Registration number 21891

DIMENSIONS

Length overall	692 ft / 211.2 m
Length between perpendiculars	680 ft / 207.3 m
Length on upper deck	691 ft / 210.6 m
Beam (width) of hull	83 ft / 25.3 m
Breadth across the paddle-boxes	118 ft / 36 m
Depth from main deck to keel	58 ft / 17.7 m
Depth of hull	83 ft / 25.3 m
Draught at that weight	30 ft 6 in. / 9.3 m
Draught unladen	15½ ft / 4.7 m
Weight of ship with machinery, coal, cargo, etc.	26,000 tons
Registered tonnage	13,343 tons
Gross tonnage	18,915 tons
Speed	14 knots / 26 kph

HULL

Plates of iron used in the construction of the hull	30,000
Number of rivets used in fastening the plates	3,000,000
Weight of iron used in the construction of the hull	10,000 tons
Thickness of iron plates in keel	1 inch / 2.5 cm
Thickness of iron plates in the skin	¾ inch / 1.9 cm
Thickness of iron plates in the bulkheads	½ inch / 1.3 cm
Thickness of iron deck	½ inch / 1.3 cm

CARGO

Holds	2
Length of each hold	60ft / 18.3 m
Capacity of each hold	1,000 tons
Total cargo capacity of ship	6,000 tons
Coal ports for loading	20

FITTINGS

Decks	4
Masts	6
Boats	20
Number of screw steamers abaft paddle boxes (planned but never built)	2
Length of screw steamers	100 ft / 30.5 m
Canvas under sail	6,500 sq yds / 5,435 m²
Number of anchors	10
Length of chain cable 800 fathoms	4,800ft / 1463 m
Weight of anchors, cables, etc.	253 tons

ACCOMMODATION

Full passenger capacity	4,000
1st class	800
2nd class	2,000
3rd class	1,200
Total accommodation	4,000
Number of saloons	10
Length of principal saloon	62ft / 19 m
Width of ditto	36ft / 11 m
Height of ditto	12ft / 4 m
Length of berths	14ft / 4 m
Width of ditto	10ft / 3 m
Height of ditto	7ft / 2 m

ENGINES AND PROPULSION

Nominal horse power of paddle engines	1,200hp / 883kw
Number of cylinders	4
Diameter of cylinders	6ft 2in / 1.9m
Length of stroke	14 ft / 4.3m
Number of boilers for paddle engines	4
Weight of each boiler	50 tons
Number of furnaces for paddle engines	40
Diameter of paddle wheels	56ft / 17m
later reduced to	50ft / 15.2m 30 floats, 13ft / 4m long 3ft / 0.9m deep
Nominal horse power of screw engines	1,600 / 1,777kw
Number of cylinders	4
Diameter of cylinders	7 ft / 2.1m
Length of stroke	4 ft / 1.2m
Number of boilers for screw engines	6
Weight of each boiler	57 tons
Number of furnaces for screw engines	72
Screw propeller	4-bladed,
diameter	24 ft / 7.3m
pitch	44 ft / 13.4m
Number of auxiliary engines	2, to keep the keep the propeller turning slowly when the ship was riding at anchor
Number of donkey engines	10, two per boiler room to supply boilers with water and work bilge and fire pumps
Nominal horse power of donkey engines	40hp / 29kw

MASTS

Number of masts: 6

	LENGTH	DIAMETER AT CENTRE
Monday	172ft / 52.4m	2¾ ft / 0.8m Fore-and-aft rigged
Tuesday	216ft / 65.8m	3½ ft / 1.1m Square rigged
Wednesday	255ft / 77.7m	3½ ft / 1.1m Square rigged
Thursday	216ft / 65.8m	3½ ft / 1.1m Fore-and-aft rigged, capable of carrying square sails
Friday	188ft / 57.3m	2¾ ft / 0.8m Fore-and-aft rigged
Saturday	164ft / 50m	2¾ ft / 0.8m Fore-and-aft rigged

Material of masts: iron, except Saturday (wood because of the proximity of the steering compass)

Lower yards

LENGTH	DIAMETER AT CENTRE
126 ft / 38.4m	2½ ft / 0.7m

Stays: 7½ in / 19m wire rope (except on Saturday, where they were hemp)

Bibliography

Banbury, Philip, *Shipbuilders of the Thames and Medway.*
Newton Abbot: David & Charles, 1971.

Baynes, Ken and Pugh, Francis, *The Art of the Engineer.*
Guildford: Lutterworth Press, 1981.

Beaver, Patrick, *The Big Ship: Brunel's Great Eastern, a pictorial history.*
London: Hugh Evelyn Ltd, 1969.

Brindle, Steven, *Brunel: the man who built the world.*
London: Weidenfeld & Nicholson, 2005.

Brunel, Isambard, *The Life of Isambard Kingdom Brunel, civil engineer.*
London: Longmans, Green & Co., 1870.

Buchanan, R. Angus, *Brunel: the life and times of Isambard Kingdom Brunel.*
London: Hambledon & London, 2002.

Dugan, James, *The Great Iron Ship.*
London: Hamish Hamilton, 1953.

Glover, Bill, *Great Eastern.* http://atlantic-cable.com/Cableships/GreatEastern
accessed December 2014.

Kershman, Andrew, *London's Monuments.*
London Metro Publications, 2013.

Lambert, Andrew, *John Scott Russell – ships, science
and scandal in the age of transition.*
International Journal for the History of Engineering
& Technology, 81: 1, 60-78. 2011